27/5/77

To
Daddy
Wishing you a Happy
Birthday
all our love,
Dorothy,

Many Happy Returns and
Best Wishes on your
Birthday
Sammy.

Just Like it Was

Just Like it Was

Memoirs of the Mittel East

Harry Blacker

Illustrations by the Author

Vallentine, Mitchell – London

First published in Great Britain in 1974 by
VALLENTINE, MITCHELL & CO. LTD.,
67 Great Russell Street,
London WC1B 3BT

Copyright © 1974 Harry Blacker

ISBN 0 85303 178 9

Designed by Harold King

Printed in Great Britain by
Unwin Brothers Limited
The Gresham Press
Old Woking Surrey

To the Memory of

DR. NORMAN LEVY
PETER AND JACK GREYSTOKE
DR. HARRY BARRON
LOUIS AND HETTY METZ
DAVID SILVER

★   ★   ★

To my dear Harry and Kitty Garland who were present the night my memoirs were born; to Barnet Litvinoff, writer and good friend, who guided my pen into a semblance of lucidity and with infinite patience corrected some of my worst errors; to Michael Freedland, whose Radio London programme 'You Don't Have To Be Jewish' brought my memoirs to the attention of thousands of listeners; and to Simon Blumenfeld, author, critic, editor and friend, who printed my first story.

Contents

Then and Now   12
A Bag of Bagels   15
From Russia with Bicarbonate   18
Torah for Beginners   21
In Hot Water   25
Cowboys and Indians   27
A Class of Life   31
Family by Flashlight   34
The Three 'Rs'   38
A Complement of Seasons   42
A Park Called Victoria   47
The Nut Game   50
Marriages Were Made in Heaven   53
The Seaside Beside the Sea   56
Pastoral Symphony   60
Shopping at Mrs Rubin's   64
Measure for Measure   68
Workers' Praytime   71
Beggar's Opera   74
It's Cheaper in the Lane   78
Teething Troubles   83
Live and Learn   86
Borscht for the Breadwinner   92
The Club   97
Itchy Park   100

Contents

Visiting Cards   102
Playing the Game   105
Stardust   109
Love Thy Neighbour   112
Evening In   116
The Turn   120
Polinsky's Horse   123
A Day Passes   127
Please God By Your Children   132
A Man Already   139
Party Peace   144
The Spoken Word   148
I Wish You Better   150
On the Bridge at Midnight   153
Apprentice   157
Nation Shall Speak to Nation   163
Rags to Riches   165
Running Repairs   168
Jobs for the Boys   170
Ring Up the Curtain   173
Frying Tonight   177
The Sound of Music   181
Keep Your Fingers Crossed   188
Hearts and Flowers   190

Illustrations

Backyard Fence 13
Tramp 14
The Bagel Syndicate: Osborn Street 17
Old Man Standing at Prayer 23
Picture kindly loaned by Chaim Lipschitz, Esq.
Sabbath Night 29
Life Drawing: Nude 33
Mother as a Young Woman 35
Grandmother with my Uncle (as a child) 37
View from a Seaside Boarding-House 57
Train Leaving London Bridge Station 63
Mrs Rubin's Delicatessan 65
Old Man at Prayer 73
The Collector 77
In the Lane 81
Kitchen Interior: Homework 87
My Mother's Sewing-Machine 89
Rooftops I 95
Local Dance Hall 108
My Sister Poses 113
Milliner at Work 115
Goodnight Sweetheart 119
Public Library Counter 129
Washing Line 131
Father as a Young Man 135

Illustrations

Grandfather and Grandson   141
Party Night   145
Self-portrait   152
Street Missionary   155
Signing on at the Labour Exchange   159
Picture kindly loaned by Alfred Diamond, OBE, JP
The Jewish Reading Room, Whitechapel   160–161
Trying On   172
Life Drawing   175
Frying Tonight   179
Rooftops II   192

Then and Now

Then

The Mittel East of my childhood encompassed the districts of Bethnal Green, Hackney, Shoreditch, Whitechapel and Stepney. Until I was fifteen years old my parents lived in a flat on the second floor of a terraced house in Gibraltar Walk, a turning off the main Bethnal Green Road. The house was dark, dingy, and had a shop at street-level. During our tenancy, this shop was in turn a decorative plaster works supplying local cabinetmakers with garland-motifs to be applied to the panels of wardrobes; a junk shop run by a mental character called Lightning, for no apparent reason except that this infuriated him; and finally an old-clothes emporium, whose owner, a tetchy old lady, bickered constantly with all and sundry.

Our flat was up two flights of bare-board creaky wooden stairs which, despite the ceaseless use of disinfectant by my mother and the tenant on the first floor, always smelled of cats.

We lived in three rooms: two of them were bedrooms, the third, our kitchen-cum-dining room, where the oil smell of my mother's sewing machine mingled with the odour of fresh baked bread and the steam rising up from newly washed underclothes drying in front of the fire.

School was five minutes walk away along the Columbia Road and most of my friends lived just around the corner.

The time was during and shortly after the War to end all wars.

★ ★ ★

Now

The Mittel East of my memoirs is no more. It was murdered by Hitler's Luftwaffe and quietly buried by the march of time and redevelopment. In the old native quarter the bug-infested tenements have been transformed into hygienic centrally-heated flats. The scruffy soot-scattered backyards in which our mothers hung out the family wash each Sunday morning have been miraculously changed into well-tended lawns ornamented by award-winning but obscure sculpture. Time has healed the angst between immigrant Jew and gentile. Time has also eroded the love and camaraderie that once drew neighbour close to neighbour.

In the suburbs of London and in seaside Sussex towns, the erstwhile natives of the Mittel East pass their declining years. I well remember them in their vigorous prime, and in the act of remembrance include the memory of my mother and father, who lived to provide for my future and whose untimely passing severed my last direct link with the Mittel East which I loved.

A Bag
of Bagels

Sweet and sour summed up the flavour of life. They also reflected its gastronomic preferences. Native-owned delicatessens were a veritable cornucopia of tasty tidbits. Pickled herring beringed with onions, sour cream, soft cheese, black and green olives, dutch cucumbers, sauerkraut, sweet cabbage and appetite-whetting smoked salmon cut paper-thin and sold by the ounce. All these delicacies and more were eaten on buttered-rye bread with the Bakers' Union paperseal on the crust.

Almost without exception, every home in the quarter ate its daily quota of rolls (with or without poppy-seeds), platzels (with or without onion), and countless rings of crisp, crunchy bagels. The acute indigestion that invariably followed their consumption was accepted as an occupational hazard, quickly ameliorated by a spoonful of bicarbonate of soda in water. Each native group had its special source of supply, where the cream was creamier, the bagels fresher, and the smoked salmon like a foretaste of heaven on earth.

★   ★   ★

'If you are going for a walk', said my mother, 'buy for me a sixpence bagel.'

I always enjoyed these sudden forays for food, and, having kissed her

15

goodbye, would run off on my errand. Being a native of the Mittel East, I knew where to go for the freshest, crispiest bagels you had ever tasted. There were, in fact, two groups we patronised. One traded on the pavement in front of Bloom's salt beef emporium, the other operated by Schewzik's Russian Vapour Baths in Brick Lane.

It was towards the latter that I made my way. In front of the gateway to the baths and in the holy shadow of the Machzike Hadass synagogue, the bagel syndicate hawked its wares.

Seated on upturned orange-boxes, enveloped in voluminous overcoats that came up to their ears and knitted caps that came down over them, were two of the most shapeless women I had ever seen. Their faces were set in a permanent grimace, like that of a rubber doll's when squeezed between thumb and forefinger. The bulging sacks of bagels pressed up against their slipper-shod feet, looked like an integral part of their bodies. Here, in all their glory, were the bagel queens of the Lane. Apart from beady eyes that flickered from side to side like metronomes, the only sign of life they displayed was a gutteral cry of 'Bagel, bagel', which they emitted at regular intervals like the fog-siren of a lightship. Should you in your unforgivable ignorance deign to pass them by without making a purchase, a duet of deep-throated Yiddish curses would follow in your wake until you were out of earshot. But any purchase, however small, would immediately put you in the running for a long life and a certain place in heaven when the time came (not for 120 years!) for the Angel of Death to gather you in his arms.

My normal strategy was to walk past them, whistling casually, thus encouraging a full broadside of their combined invective. Suddenly I would turn back and buy my bagels. Their recovery-rate was fantastic. Without pausing for breath, the curses would run smoothly into blessings as my six pennyworth was counted and put into a crinkly paper bag.

A hang-dog weasel-faced man wearing a shabby once-black overcoat, and a flat cap, would arrive and stock up their depleted sacks from a perambulator, which he wheeled through the streets direct from the bakehouse. I never discovered whether he was one of their husbands, a son, or familiar: they never exchanged anything but curses in my hearing. In fact, if it was not for the bag of still warm bagels in my hand at the time, I would have passed him off as a figment of my youthful imagination. However, the bagels were always oven-fresh, geometric in their roundness, and shining like a good deed in an iniquitous world.

From Russia with Bicarbonate

Until I was fifteen my family lived in Bethnal Green. In those days the Mittel East was a conglomeration of narrow, cobbled streets, terraced houses, cat-smelling tenements, and gas-lit cabinet-making workshops. In Virginia Road, a sawmill banshee howled through planks of wood. Across the way Abrams the Goy, a french polisher by trade, applied his oils and varnishes and when drunk on Saturday nights, beat his wife unmercifully. On the corner of Gibraltar Walk Jones' dairy supplied milk direct from the cows they housed in an adjoining stable; it was ladled into the jug still warm. A minute's walk away, Mrs Rubin's grocery and delicatessen provided smoked salmon and schmaltz herring by the barrel full. She recorded all non-cash purchases on the back of a blue-sugar bag with the stub of a carpenter's pencil. Later my parents moved to West Ham (the Far East), but it was in the Mittel East that life unfolded for me based on an Anglo-Russian pattern. Particularly so was the food we ate: gefilte fish, tzimas, calves foot jelly, ornamented with egg-rings, cabbage borscht, and the hundred other delicacies that graced our tables. It was the Sabbath chollant that marked the passing weeks, not the milkman's calendar.

★   ★   ★

On Friday after school, my mother said to me: 'Go take the chollant to the baker shop. You can play after. So make quick'.

Chollant was the traditional Sabbath meal eaten by most native families in the Mittel East. The concoction was a melange of meat, potatoes, butter-beans, onions, kishkeh, kugel and hope. For the uninitiated, kishkeh vaguely resembles a kosher haggis. It consisted of a pale outer skin or casing, about a foot long and sewn at one end. This was stuffed with a mixture of flour, meal, grated onion and fat, seasoned with salt, pepper and paprika. The open end was then stitched up, and the completed kishkeh carefully placed in the pot to allow for expansion. The kugel (German for bullet), looked like an anaemic cannon-ball. The recipe varied from family to family and depended on their tolerance of bulk and the state of their digestive tract. The basic formula included fat, flour, grebenes or fried onion. It had a rubber-like consistency, and when eaten in large portions produced a state of euphoria which, when combined with the kishkeh, resulted in instant dyspepsia.

All this was carefully arranged in a large copper saucepan brought over from Russia by my mother, covered with water and enclosed in a clean white cloth tied into position with string. It was then carried to the nearest bakehouse, where for a small consideration (about two pence), the baker would put the pan in the oven to cook until the following midday. Every native baker kept his oven going for this purpose which, apart from obliging his customers, took in quite a bit of easy cash in the process. Our nearest was at the Brick Lane end of Gossett Street, where, sandwiched between Lazarus the barber and Cooper's dairy, Mrs Schwartz kept her tiny shop. You walked up three stone steps and were immediately tantalised by the smell of fresh bread and cinnamon spices. On Fridays the shelves were stocked with egg-glazed chollas liberally sprinkled with poppy-seed. Here also were large black metal trays covered with golden-brown round biscuits, jam tarts, cinnamon-sugared rusks (ideal for dunking), and the inevitable swollen yeast cakes, scarcely contained by their tins.

I staggered the quarter mile up the road towards Mrs Schwartz's bakehouse, joined in my pilgrimage by Hymie from downstairs and Morry who lived next door. Like the three kings bearing gifts we made our way to the baker's Bethlehem. Mrs Schwartz, a tall austere widow, with her hair piled up on her head like one of her own cottage loaves, greeted us by name in Yiddish.

'Put down the chollants inside by the oven,' she commanded.

Despite her forbidding appearance, Mrs Schwartz would give us a hunk of yeast cake, or an onion platzel, to be consumed on the homeward journey, together with a metal number token (which was not). The counterpart of the token was attached to the handle of our saucepan. Come Saturday after synagogue, the same procession formed up outside the bakehouse to collect the pots whose odour made one faint with hunger. In the bakehouse, its concrete floor covered by flour-dust like a winter's snow-shower, chollants were being withdrawn from the brick oven by the baker. He used a long wooden paddle, the flat end of which was slid under the saucepans at the far end of the oven.

As each one appeared, he would call out the number on the metal token tied to the handle and the respective pot was claimed by its owner. When my number came up, I handed the baker the token, and collected the chollant. The white linen cloth had turned sepia in the oven's heat, but the lap-lap of gravy which could be heard with each movement of the pot, indicated that the chollant had not 'dried out' during its ordeal by fire. Had it done so, not only would the meal be regarded as a gastronomic failure, but it would also have led to a bitter and spirited verbal battle between my mother and Mrs Schwartz. Inevitably, whether mother won the argument about the oven being overheated or not, I would somehow become responsible for the mishap. With dire consequences.

With gravy splashing around at each step we reached home, where the top cloth was untied and removed to reveal the delicious brown chollant in all its succulent goodness. How its haunting flavour filled the room as kugel and kishkeh were excavated from the pot as if by an obstetrician making a forceps delivery. Soon the contents were served to everyone's satisfaction. We tucked into our helpings until not a butterbean remained. This was followed by glasses of lemon tea served from the shining samovar and drunk with refined sucking noises through a piece of sugar held between the teeth. Afterwards, my sister helped with the washing-up. Our parents retired to sleep until teatime. I just sat with a stupefied seraphic grin on my face, burping quietly.

Torah for
Beginners

Most of the natives in my sector of the Mittel East came from Russia.
They brought with them their loves, traditions, favourite saucepans,
samovars, and an instinctive respect for learning. They built tiny synagogues in the side streets and founded Hebrew classes for their little ones.
Every afternoon following school the children would be served a hasty
tea and then run off reluctantly to cheder. Here, in ill-lit overcrowded
classrooms, short-tempered, yarmelke-covered rabbis would teach Hebrew, with a book in one hand and a cane in the other. Punishment was
dished out liberally. Woe betide the unfortunate who failed to grasp the
meaning of a phrase, or did not readily recognise the shape of a letter.
Tears and lamentations were threaded through the Sh'ma Yisroel like
metallic thread through a Torah vestment. Despite this, we learned to
read and write Hebrew. I have never forgotten the poems and songs
driven into my subconscious by a well-meaning but sadistic rabbi. Even
today, I surprise myself recalling chapter and verse from some obscure
passage in the Talmud.

*   *   *

One Sunday morning my mother said to me, 'Hurry up and finish the
breakfast or you will be late for cheder'. Every day, excepting Fridays,

I was compelled to attend Hebrew classes. Normal day school would finish at four-thirty and after a hasty tea, I would be packed off for religious teaching. My father was a cabinet-maker from Russia and had helped found and build a synagogue in the Mittel East known as the United Workman's Congregation. After a hard day's work, he would come home, eat his dinner and then go off to the site, where he and many other craftsmen worked until midnight making seats, cupboards, doors, an ark and bima for the proposed synagogue. In time, when this task was completed, a Hebrew class was opened in the rooms above.

About fifty children were crammed into each tiny room. The only light at night came from one incandescent gas mantle which hissed and popped incessantly. My rabbi looked like a Christ figure in an El Greco painting. He came from Russia via a short sojourn in Glasgow. This gave his broken English a Scottish flavour. When I had mastered this stage of our communication, I began to learn Hebrew.

In between occasional thumps on the head, rapped knuckles and notes of complaint to my mother, I slowly absorbed the intricacies of Hebrew grammar, its left-to-right calligraphy, and the geometric vowels that adorned each word. The time came when I could read and write without difficulty, parse verbs, compose stories, all in a language that, at the outset, had seemed impossible to master.

We sat on long wooden forms, with a plank-like desk attached. As many pupils as possible were crammed onto each unit. Writing could only be done by arrangement with one's immediate neighbours. The gangway between the forms was so narrow that normal walking was impossible. Most of us bore permanent bruises on our knees throughout our cheder life.

About ten girls were included on our roll call and strategically placed in a group across the room. This made the seats near them extremely popular. The young Lotharios in our midst would be the first to arrive every evening in order to take up favourite positions. Notes were passed and hair pulled until the rabbi's eagle eye would catch a culprit red-handed. This meant dire punishment by cane or swift retribution in the shape of a large bible brought down none too gently on one's head. Most of the pupils within striking distance of our rabbi were soon recognisable by the closeness of their ears to their shoulders.

Despite the sturm and drang of cheder life, we learned much. My greatest moment of triumph was when I found myself thinking in

Hebrew! Barmitzvah presented no difficulties; coaching was unnecessary. Any lad in my class could, at a moment's notice, be called up to the Torah and read the portion with ease. The only extra effort for a thirteen-year-old was the committing to memory in Yiddish, English and Hebrew of a rather long and sentimental speech which was turned on and off like a tap at the family dinner usually held on the immediate Sunday following the Barmitzvah ceremony.

As I grew more proficient in my studies, the rabbi ceased to be a menacing ogre. He would offer me what were no doubt tantalising rewards in his eyes, opportunities for extra study. On Saturday afternoons when my less fortunate comrades went off to watch a football match or 'bunk in' at the local cinema, I would be grappling with Gemmorah or Mishna. This extra tuition was free. The weekly pittance which my parents paid to the collector for my teaching covered a period from Sunday morning to week nights, Monday to Thursday inclusive.

I also visited the rabbi in his home under duress from my mother (no rabbi, no pictures). Together we would chat away in Hebrew, read from the Talmud, discuss and retranslate the week's Sidra into our own words. This went on until I was sixteen years of age and included written homework almost nightly. Apart from all this, I had my normal school work to do; but we survived. Many of my classmates went on to the Jews College and became rabbis. I found other distractions.

In Hot Water

Houses and tenements in my neighbourhood were old and bug-infested. Stray cats abounded and whenever the front door opened, a flurry of dust and paper was blown in from the street. A never-ending onslaught of soap, carbolic and sulphur helped to keep the places habitable.

The landlord was a nebulous ogre who functioned through his agent. It was the agent who determined whether a flat needed decorating, the lavatory a new seat, or the drains unstopping. Hygiene was at a premium, paid off in ceaseless sweat and manhours. A three-storied house was shared by three families. The passageway and first flight of stairs were scrubbed each week in turn by one's mother or elder sister. This was the unwritten law, and woe betide the family who ignored it. Day to day washing was performed under the cold tap of the kitchen sink. Hot water could only be obtained by putting the kettle on the fire, and bathrooms were places you read about in books and magazines. Every Friday the older children were sent off to the Council baths for an 'all-over' clean up. The little ones were dealt with by Mama in a zinc bath in front of the fire.

When I was adult enough to cross the main road unattended I joined the weekly procession to the Baths.

*   *   *

On Fridays during winter when I came home from school, my mother would order me: 'Go now to Cheshire Street and don't come back late for the Sabbath'.

In the brown paper bag that my mother had prepared for me, I carried a change of underwear, a towel, a face-cloth and a large bar of Lifebuoy soap. Not the effeminate substance that goes by the name today, but of an honest-to-goodness floor scrubbing quality that reeked of carbolic and removed most of one's skin with the dirt.

I also packed a handful of domestic soda which, while softening the water, when combined with the aforementioned soap made skin-shedding a cert.

On arrival at my destination, I paid the requisite penny admission fee and entered the bath area, where I sat on a well-scrubbed white wood seat to await my turn in one of about twenty bath cubicles that filled the room. The air was full of steam, singing, and the plaintive cries of already immersed customers who yelled 'Hot water number fifteen' or 'Please some cold water in number three'. When my turn was nigh, I followed the attendant, who, because of my tender years, always treated me in cavalier fashion.

The cubicle had just been vacated. With a spanner key he turned on the cold tap, and then thoroughly cleansed the bath using a long-handled broom dipped in liquid disinfectant. Then, in a cloud of steam, on went the hot water, gushing like a miniature Niagara. Having doled out the hot, the cold tap was given a turn. I tested the water with my hand and said, 'That's all right, mister.' The door would then be closed on me with a cautionary 'Don't be all day abaht it.'

Having put in the soda, placed the soap and flannel in the wire rack provided, I hurriedly undressed and stepped into the bath. This was invariably scalding hot. It was years later that I discovered that the elbow was a far more reliable temperature tester than one's hand. Soon my voice would join the chorus of supplicants with an appeal for 'More cold water number fourteen, please!' until the angry attendant complied with my request. Every cubicle had its number painted on both sides of the door.

Thus a pleasant fifteen minutes or so were spent in bathing and conversing with friends in other cubicles, until the attendant would run amok and without a word of warning, empty all the baths from the outside, leaving you high if not dry, like a barge in a canal lock. Reluctantly I would step out onto the damp duckboards and vigorously dry myself. I then put on the clean underwear and parcelled up the flannel, soap and soiled linen in the brown bag my mother had given me.

Pausing for a brief moment to comb my hair before the circular mirror bearing an advertisement for a well-known disinfecting fluid, I would brave the attendant's wrath by yelling at the top of my voice and rush out of the building towards home and the Sabbath.

26

Cowboys and Indians

From Monday to Friday life was grim and earnest. My father, a craftsman cabinet-maker of the old school, left home for his workshop at the crack of dawn. He returned at night when we, the children, were tucked up in bed. My mother, besides carrying out the daily chores of cooking, scrubbing, shopping and dealing with the family wash, also made most of the clothes we wore. From our bedroom we could hear her sewing machine tack-tacking away, running up shirts and dresses until father would say 'Time for bed'.

Only at weekends did the struggle subside. The lighting of the Sabbath candles heralded an uneasy truce. Saturday night was its peak. My father, rested and in good humour, gave us our 'spending money' and would pour himself a glass of whisky. Comfortably seated by the fire in his own-made rocking-chair, he delved through the weekly accumulation of Yiddish papers, which he purchased from Bernstein's shop in Virginia Road. It was then that my sister and I waited expectantly for my mother's decision. Would she decide on a visit to relations or a trip to the cinema?

★   ★   ★

On some Saturday evenings my mother would say, 'Wash your face and hands quick—we are going to the pictures'. In a flurry of soap and water my sister and I would comply with her request and then, with coats buttoned to the neck, walk down the dark stairway that led from our second-floor flat to the street. The cinema we usually patronised was in Chicksand Street, a narrow dingy turning diagonally opposite Flower and Dean Street, still shuddering from the memory of Jack the Ripper. We crossed Bethnal Green Road at Haltrecht's corner and walked through the odiferous Brick Lane market. Here in the light of hissing naphtha flares, late night shoppers gathered round the fruit and vegetable stalls making their last-minute purchases for the weekend. Soon we reached the railway arch with its large wall opening like a gateway to hell. Whenever a train passed on the track below, steam and smoke would belch out of the hole reducing visibility to a minimum. Beyond this arch a couple of hawkers sold pineapple chunks and it became the custom on these special outings for mother to buy us each a piece to be eaten en route.

Eventually Chicksand Street came into sight and we rushed off to take our place in the queue. My mother would recognise old friends and chat away in Yiddish whilst my sister and I exchanged our spending money for massive bags of peanuts, still warm from their on-the-spot roasting. By twos and threes, the queue dwindled as room became available in the auditorium, and soon it was our turn to be ushered in. On the diminutive screen, the 'big picture' had already started. Under it, curtained off from the main audience, Miss Daniels, a heavily made up brunette, played a piano accompaniment to the tragic drama that flickered overhead. The heat was terrific. A perpetual buzz of conversation mingled with the crackle of peanut shells that littered the floor like snow in winter. Every step in any direction crunched.

Having found three seats together, we removed our coats and sat back to enjoy the programme. Nearby, children were reading the titles out loud for the benefit of their foreign parents. Some even translated the words directly into Yiddish. Babies cried, kids were slapped, and an endless procession to the 'ladies and gents' was greeted by outraged cries of 'Siddown'. Only the screen was silent. It was here, and in other cinemas like it, that I saw Pearl White, Eddie Polo (in person), Houdini, Charlie Chaplin, Fatty Arbuckle, Buster Keaton, Ben Turpin, Pola Negri, Chester Conklin, The Keystone Cops, Nazimova, Louise Fazenda, Harold Lloyd, The Gish Sisters, Mary Pickford, and a host of other luminaries in a fast-developing cinema world.

No air-conditioning disturbed the fug of cigarette smoke and perspiring humanity. From time to time an usher would walk up and down the aisles spraying the air with a perfumed disinfectant that made you smart if you got an eyeful. At the end of each reel, a slide appeared stating 'end of part one' or 'two', or whatever it happened to be. Resuming projection, the operator usually missed the screen by a foot or so above or below. This was greeted with booing and a slow hand-clap punctuated with loud cries of 'Higher' or 'Lower' until all was well. The peanut crackle and general hubbub was resumed, and the audience settled back in their seats for further enjoyment.

When it was all over and 'the end' faded out Miss Daniels played a very spirited National Anthem, somewhat drowned by the noise of shells crackling underfoot as we stood in respect before the portraits of George V and Queen Mary spanning the silver screen. Attendants walked round and woke up those customers who, still under the influence of the post-Chollant barbiturate, had comfortably snored through the complete programme. Still excitedly chattering about Cowboys or Comedians we had seen in the show, my mother, sister and I would arrive home where father had prepared hot cocoa and buttered cholla for us so that we could go to bed soon after.

A Class of Life

Fine Art had no place in the Mittel East. Economic pressures made this field of culture inaccessible to the natives. Colour found its way into the homes of the people via the milkman's calendar, or the pre-Raphaelite transfers on the giant ornamental vases that were exchanged for blue trading stamps. The art that did smuggle itself across the border, was sentimental in flavour and lush in colour. Love's idylls; shepherds, sheep and sunsets; swordplay in costume (for he had spoken lightly of a women's honour), and the inevitable child Samuel gazing heavenwards toward the fly-specked ceiling of the room. But the children of the quarter were beginning to show signs of creative ability, drawing with chalk and paint the dreams that were growing inside them. Despite the lack of parental enthusiasm for this cultural manifestation, many of these dedicated tyros did emerge as important artists with the inspiration and craftsmanship to realise their urges. At the age of eight, it became apparent that I could draw. Nine years later, I was able to do something about it.

*   *   *

'Eat now, before you go to night school', my mother said to me.

I was seventeen years of age and had just enrolled in the art class of our local institute. Two nights a week after work, I would make a hasty supper, then dash off to the school, which was about a mile away. We were all dedicated and in deadly earnest. The teacher, a sculptor by profession and looking strangely like a red-headed Sherlock Holmes, fanned our enthusiasm to fever pitch, making the interval between lessons an arid wilderness. I could scarcely wait for the night to come so that I could return to my paints and crayons. We drew still lifes and shaky figure drawings in heroic attitudes glowing with colour and executed with primitive draughtsmanship.

By the second term, most of us had settled down to a steady grind, accepting our teacher's praise or criticism with open minds. Our work began to improve as our awareness increased. My particular bent was toward mural painting. I rushed where angels feared to tread, and found myself in heaven. Still floating on the crest of my creative wave, I decorated the walls of my bedroom in the native quarter with a seaside panorama graced with voluptuous beauties in bathing costume. Blue skies punctured by fleecy clouds covered two walls, and a Mediterranean sea (a triumph of my imagination, since the only sea I knew washed the stony beaches of Hastings), sparkled in the golden sunshine.

When the work was completed, I invited by father to examine the masterpiece. Until that moment of truth, he was completely unaware of my effort. He climbed the narrow twisting stairway to my attic bedroom, and stood in the open doorway the better to take in the prospect before him. Palette in hand, I modestly awaited his judgment. He put on his steel-rimmed spectacles, looked around the room and said, 'It will take three coats of distemper to cover that lot when we decorate'. I knew Michelangelo had his tough moments as well as his triumphs. I suffered in silence, and continued with my studies.

'It's time you went to a life class', my teacher said one evening. This was to be a milestone in my career, and a millstone around my enthusiasm. My parents lived in the Mittel East. No one would have called it a particularly enlightened existence. Many of the prejudices they practised were bred into them by my unknown but revered grandparents. How could I explain the need for drawing naked men and women in terms of my artistic development? Nevertheless, it had to be done. In a moment of inspiration, I told them that I was going to study figures. This was a happy solution to the problem, and left my conscience clear. It was several years later that my father remarked on the fact, that despite my prolonged study of figures, I seemed strangely incapable of solving the simplest mathematical sum. A fact which I never denied.

Family by Flashlight

On the bug-stained walls of the houses were the genealogical charts of the natives who lived in them. Almost every room in the quarter had its share of family portraits, past and present, carefully mounted under glass and lovingly framed in ornate mahogany and gilt frames. Many of the pictures came from villages in Russia and Poland, where the photographer's business acumen outweighed his technical know-how. Already an insidious fading process was transforming the once-sharp unsmiling images into austere sepia ghosts. At intervals, usually associated with outstanding ceremonial or catastrophic events, the family, dressed in their Sabbath best and smelling strongly of mothballs and brilliantine, would hie themselves to the local studio, where, in a flash of magnesium powder, the moment of joy or sadness would be recorded for all time. The results were preserved in albums or displayed with fierce pride on top of the upright grand which graced many a native's front parlour. In time, an enlargement would be ordered and paid for in weekly instalments. When framed, it would be formally hung on any available wallspace the room happened to afford. It was the album, however, that kept the record up-to-date.

*　　*　　*

'Clear away the comics from the table,' my mother said to me. 'Guests are coming to tea.'

Sunday afternoon was visiting time in the Mittel East. Most of the bread-winners in the quarter worked a five-and-a-half-day week which ended around midday on the Sabbath. They came home, had a meal, then slept for the rest of the day. Sunday was the day of indulgence: breakfast at a civilised hour; a quiet uninterrupted read of the Yiddish

Zeitungen in the rocking-chair by the window; a mooch round the neighbourhood market in search of bargains.

It was on Sunday afternoons that the natives exchanged visits, to partake of tea and home-baked delicacies and to catch up with the events of the week. It was also the time for ritually turning the pages of the family album.

The album was usually about the size and thickness of a volume of the *Encyclopedia Britannica*. Its covers were padded and velvet lined, the pages gilt-edged and firmly enclosed by an intricate brass clasp that clicked like a rifle shot when fastened. Within its ornamental heart the album sheltered the likenesses of grandparents from Russia, uncles from Poland, cousins from South Africa, and innumerable landsleit who had befriended my parents since their coming to the Mittel East.

After tea, the white tablecloth would be brushed for crumbs, folded and put away in the sideboard drawer. It was immediately replaced by a green-plush, bobble-edged de luxe model that was our pride and joy. The album, which usually reposed on a shelf beneath a flowerpot stand, would be reverently removed and gently deposited onto the table. This was the signal for guests to take up viewing positions around my mother, who slowly turned the pages, delivering an informal lecture on the life and times of each portrait. Both the order of appearance and the mono-logue remained unchanged for years. As time went on, and the album was stuffed to overflowing, new pictures were placed between the pages in strict chronological order, and the commentary amended to embrace them. Every so often the page would reveal a cousin in a suit obviously too small for him, or wearing a rakishly tilted boater. This would produce a burst of spontaneous laughter and a fierce eye-wiping operation from an overcome aunt. A procession of leg-of-mutton sleeves, saucy bustles, corsetted waists, frilly furbelows and cottage-loaf hairdos went by, each one given her fair due by my mother. The men of our family were invariably photographed with their left hand resting on an adjacent pedestal or chair-back, whilst their right hand held back their jackets to reveal solid Albert watch chains afloat with Masonic charms and clasps. They had Gladstone collars, tight-tapered trousers, buffalo-horn mous-taches, pomaded centre-partings, and malacca canes.

The highlight of the weekly showing, surveyed always to an accom-paniment of oohs and ahs, was the baby section. Child after child of indeterminate sex was immortalised tummy-down in the nude on a sheepskin rug. Their cherub-mouthed, podgy faces were topped by finger-waved ringlets, the prototypes for a hundred milkmen's calendars. Memories would be revived and recounted. This was the moment for listener participation. The cutting of a first tooth; a haircut; infant school; barmitzvah; measles (God will protect us); death (he should rest in peace); she is getting married soon (Mazeltov).

The pages were turned and time passed pleasantly until the children grew fretful. Fights were nipped in the bud, bottoms slapped and peace restored. Our visitors thanked Mother for the lovely tea and went off in the dusk. The album was closed after it had been ascertained that all the photographs were present and correctly affixed by their cornerpieces. Finally, the clasp was clicked into place and the whole ceremoniously lifted from the table and lowered onto its resting-place, a velvet-covered mausoleum of our family's living as well as its dead.

The Three 'Rs'

Education or attendance at school for the young was compulsory. From the age of five, children of either sex took their first reluctant steps through the school gate marked 'Mixed Infants', where for the first week or two they were dragged screaming through its grimy portals by mothers determined to give their beloved kiddies a chance to learn.

From the outset of his or her entry into this strange world away from mama's loving care, the child was subject to stern discipline, a necessary precaution, since the teacher often presided over classes of 50 or even 60 pupils, most of them vociferously bewailing their fate and anxious to get back to the familiar surroundings of home. In time, the realisation that school was inevitable asserted itself in the minds of the little ones, who settled down to the routine with commendable results.

★   ★   ★

'Today' said mother to me, 'you are going to school.' I was five years old at the time and had been suitably conditioned for this momentous occasion by the gift of a halfpenny spending money for sweets, a new suit made by mother a week earlier, and the shearing of my beautiful curls by Issy the barber, who gave me a toy pistol and caps in fair exchange for the tears I shed during the operation. Until that eventful morning, the bell calling the faithful to school was just another sound that filtered into our second floor flat mingling with the milkman's yodel and the rattle of steel-rimmed wheels of the baker's barrow on the cobblestoned road-way of the street below. For the next seven years this steady morning clangour was to be the cause of bolted breakfasts and angry recrimination over not being awakened in time to 'eat a proper breakfast'. But on this special day in my young life the immediate future was taken up with my obvious reluctance to forsake the warmth and comfort of home for the mysterious place in nearby Columbia Road called school.

Tearfully clutching my mother's hand, I was led down the stairs to the street and dragged screaming all the way to the 'Mixed Infants', where my cries joined those of other children in the same situation and of a similar disposition.

Mother wiped away my tears, blew my nose, combed my hair, and put a white paper bag containing two slices of buttered bread into my hand. 'For lunch' she said. We then entered the main hall, which was reached by a flight of concrete steps. Some premonition of their malev-olence caused me to break into a renewed bout of weeping and wailing, as if I already knew that my knees would be lacerated a hundred times on their gritty texture.

Once in the vastness of the school hall, I was kissed by mother and handed over to Miss Chick. 'She is going to be your teacher' my mother told me in Yiddish. All around me, mothers were tearing themselves away from the clutching hands of their soon-to-be-abandoned children. In later years, I was reminded of the occasion by a drawing of Gustave Doré's illustrating a scene from 'Paradise Lost'. Here too, the victims writhed and screamed in torment and anguish.

About fifty of us were eventually separated from the mass and shep-herded into a classroom furnished with tiny chairs and tables. One by one, we were told to sit down and fold our arms until instructed to do otherwise. So there we were, strangers in a strange and unfamiliar place, missing mother's comforting reassurance, and giving vent to our mis-givings by sobbing and crying our little hearts out.

Suddenly, teacher rang a handbell and said, 'When I ring this bell, everyone must be very quiet and sit perfectly still'. Surprised by the novelty of her introduction to the order, comparative silence descended on the room. Now and again a tearful sigh would be followed by a spasmodic sob, but generally speaking we became quiet. 'Now I am going to call the register and when you hear your name, answer 'present teacher'. Miss Chick went steadily through the fifty odd names on the Roll before her and managed to elicit a 90% response. Having sorted out that problem to her satisfaction, she drew our attention to a blue rectangular box which was already placed in front of each child. 'Open the boxes and empty them on the table'. Fifty children opened fifty boxes and gazed in wonder at the contents. Long coloured matchsticks, plasticine, and sticks of coloured chalk. 'You may now play with these things until I ring the bell again. If any child wants to go to the toilet, you must raise your right hand over your head and ask to be excused.' After we realised that toilet meant lavatory, a forest of hands rose above the children, who were immediately segregated according to sex and led out of the classroom by a monitor to what we eventually discovered to be the toilets.

We played quite happily with the grey plasticine, rolling it into balls and sticking the coloured sticks into it so that it looked like a spider on stilts. After half an hour of this creative interlude, Miss Chick rang the bell and ordered the replacing of the sticks and clay and the taking up of a stick of chalk. Small wood-framed slates were then distributed and we took our first uncertain step in the world called 'Alphabet' led by Miss Chick at the blackboard. She wrote the letter 'A' and told us to try and copy it on our slates. The squeak of chalk that followed was to become a daily torment in the next few months, as letter after letter was revealed to us by the soon-to-be-adored Miss Chick. The sound of a bell in the hall outside the classroom was a signal for downing chalks and being led into the playground, crocodile-fashion, where we took stock of our situation to date as well as making use of the lavatory near a huge covered shed. Several of the children were already known to me since they were the offspring of neighbours, so we played 'touch' and 'hopping on one foot'. At the tinkle of yet another bell, we were urged to reform the crocodile and were marched back into the classroom where we were instructed to sit down, sit up and fold our arms.

Miss Chick sat down at the piano that had been moved into our room during playtime. She played a tune and sang a song about a little boy called Jack and a girl called Jill who went up a hill for a pail of water with disastrous consequences to them both.

Then line by line and note by note, she taught us our first nursery rhyme. Hitherto, the only child poems I knew were in Russian and usually ended by me being tickled under the arm or chin by my mother. Subsequently, the English counterpart turned out to be 'Walking round the garden like a teddy bear' (whatever that was). By the end of that first morning we had mastered the saga of Jack and Jill, if not the music, at concert pitch.

At noon the great bell tolled again, and we were led out into the hall where mother stood waiting for me with my overcoat. During the brief walk back to our flat I sang Jack and Jill and drew the letter 'A' in the air with my finger. This remarkable result of a mere morning's schooling impressed my mother sufficiently for her to allow me to buy 'a ha'porth of rubbish' as she called it, in the local sweetshop. Later I would relate my experiences to anyone who showed signs of interest. Meanwhile, I was now a fully registered and initiated member of the Columbia Road school 'Mixed Infants'.

A Complement of Seasons

The seasons were calculated in terms of the working and slack periods of the breadwinner. Climatic changes were incidental to full employment and often passed unnoticed in the struggle for survival. It was the young who snatched whatever pleasures the sun or snow produced, rambling through the Roman roads of Surrey in summer, or sliding down the slippery slopes of Gibraltar Walk when the ice spread its treacherous glaze on the ashphalt. For our fathers, summer meant 'short time' and reduced wages. Blue skies and fleecy clouds were strictly for the milkman's gift calendar or delivered in rhyming couplets by the lyric writers of distant USA. Winter meant work and extra money to be spent on coal or luxurious gas heaters that hissed warmth into the room through their asbestos arabesques that grew incandescent in the flame.

Spring

The slush of winter melted in the early spring sunshine and was swept into the gutters where it poured into the corner drains carrying the kerbside detritus of the quarter with it. Passover was only a week or so away and an orgy of spring cleaning was making life uncomfortable for the native males. Cupboards were turned out, scrubbed and rearranged according to the exigencies of the moment. Festival cutlery and crockery were washed, polished and placed in handy containers for easy access. Most of the housewives had already prepared the fermented beetroot that would eventually become borscht, served with meat or motza balls. The brew was kept in a small barrel which despite its tied on cover, gave off a sickly odour that permeated the house. From dark places under the stairs, bottles of home-made wine were lifted and examined for sediment or leakage. These would grace the Seder table and draw praise or adverse comment from the adult imbibers who vied with one another in their efforts to produce a perfect vintage. On outside windowsills, the potted geraniums that had miraculously survived the onslaught of winter would show signs of resurrection and spout tiny serrated leaves. Grassy lawns in local parks were besom-brushed of dead leaves and the mowers oiled and cleaned. Canaries sang; sparrows chirruped and lovers were filled with vague longings. We adolescents counted our pimples in the mirror and jostled the girls on the way home from school.

Summer

It was in the first hot flush of summer that the bugs, mercifully latent in winter, came out from behind the layers of wallpaper in the bedroom, or emerged from the joints of mattress frames where they had survived innumerable dousings of Keatings powder. A short scamper brought them within dining distance of a sleeping human that provided them with sustenance. When the situation became unbearable, the council's pest officer came to the rescue by burning acrid sulphur sticks after sealing up the doors, windows and fireplace of the room to be treated. But the bugs always came back.

Hot air would fill the tenement like a balloon and every exertion produced its attendant shower of perspiration that created an illusion of cool as it dried on the skin. When their side of the street was in shadow, people would drag out their kitchen chairs and sit in the cool, often nodding off in the lambent air.

Summer was a time for visiting the local parks or chancing your luck in the nearby Haggeston swimming bath or the more distant Pitfield Street amenities. For one penny you could enjoy an immersion in cold water, swimming being virtually impossible in the crowd. The street-corner ice cream barrow men did a roaring trade in ha'porths and penny-worths of vanilla ices that were served in cone-shaped glasses which permitted the tongue to lick up the last drip of cream. There were also massive wafers and cornets filled solid with the tongue-tingling ice held by the crisp thin biscuit or cone.

In the flat, butter and milk was kept in a bucket of cold water under the sink. Despite this, milk would go sour and the butter rancid. Nothing was wasted. The milk curds became cream cheese or eaten with butter-coated new potatoes, salt herring and spring onions.

If the finances of the family were sound, a holiday by the sea became possible during the school holidays.

Autumn

The signs of autumn were the colour changes of the virginia creeper on the local church wall. The lush cool green of summer became a fiery red and russet. Soon the leaves on the trees in the park would grow sere and flutter to the ground until all the branches were bare and looked like a print from a Japanese woodcut.

The days grew perceptibly shorter and the evenings cooler and we were glad of the comfort of our kitchen fire. The cry of the coalman was heard in the land and the hundredweight sacks of coke or coal in the cart vibrated on the cobblestones and shed their libation to the gods, which we gleaned in buckets and added to the glowing heap on the fire. Soon we would be celebrating the New Year and the solemnity of the Yom Kippur fast when the hands of the clock crawled like crippled snails towards the shofar's Grace before meals.

The terra cotta pots of geraniums huddling together on the window-sills, drooped and withered in the smoke and soot. The lamplighter did his rounds soon after tea, pole lighting the pop-popping gas lamps at the corner of Gosset Street, the resultant yellow light drawing black shadows that danced behind us as we walked. Coal bunkers were filled and bundles of wood were rescued from the sea of shavings on my father's workshop floor. This was chopped into kindling and stacked in readiness for the winter ahead. Soon the first lung-searing fog would blot out the landscape and the gunpowder explosions of the railway fog signals would sound like the distant bombardment of a besieged town.

Winter

The virgin snow that heralded the winter solstice was raped into grey slush by the native feet and swept into the drains by the road sweepers. Beads of ice were strung from the gutters under the eaves and hung in jagged daggers from the drainpipe overflow. Robin's starch sparrows picked daintily among the horse droppings and kept a weather eye open for marauding cats anxious to supplement their diet.

We were dressed in full winter kit. I wore a cap with ear-flaps that buttoned under the chin, a heavy lined overcoat which bowed my youthful shoulders and stout-soled shoes with side-buttoned gaiters that covered my legs to the knees. When I set out for school each morning, my mother would slip two hot potatoes straight from the oven into my overcoat side pockets so that I could warm my hands en route. During the lunch period, I would eat them with a pinch of pepper and salt specially wrapped in a piece of greaseproof paper for this purpose.

At this time of year visiting was reduced to a minimum. The fear of influenza was uppermost in the minds of those natives who still remembered the epidemic that followed the Great War. Doctors' surgeries were full of sneezing and coughing patients who came out of the dispensaries clutching large bottles of syrupy linctus. When the snow settled, we would build grotesque snowmen using bits of salvaged coke for the eyes and father's old top hat to give a dash of style. Inter-street snowball battles were fought with the skill and strategy of trench warfare. From the depth of shop doorways, snipers would hurl their icy missiles with deadly accuracy, their pile of ammunition pyramided at their feet like the iron cannonballs at the base of the ancient guns at the Tower.

Every evening my father would bring home a sackful of offcuts which we piled on the fire, and then luxuriated in the resultant blaze of heat. We would put a shovelful of chestnuts on the embers and bake them until the skin peeled away to reveal the floury nut which was tongue-searing hot when bitten into. The living room was kept snug and warm, but the dark passages and stairways were like ice boxes. Before we retired for the night, my father would take a hot brick out of the oven, wrap it in flannel and put it into my bed. There was a brick for each bed and it was lovely to stretch out in the comforting warmth when the wind was driving the snowflakes against the window-panes.

A Park Called Victoria

Gardens were an indulgence no landlord could afford. Most of them were transformed into roughcast unyielding grey concrete backyards which fed on the tender kneecaps of our native young. The quarter itself was overrun by a plague of unsanitary tenements and ill-lit workshops. Unexpectedly, patches of greenery in the shape of small parks and squares did survive the brick onslaught. These were protected from human depredation by threatening notices and an iron barrier of spearheaded railings. But there were larger open spaces on which no man could build. During the summer weekends, when school holidays and the heat made life unbearable for parents, they would gather food, drink, old blankets, children, and travel to the nearest park. Here, under a clear blue sky, and in comparatively fresh air, a few moments of peace could be snatched from the unceasing battle for day to day existence.

★   ★   ★

Some Sundays during the school holidays my mother would say to me, 'After breakfast, we are going to Victoria Park'. This statement was followed by an orgy of sandwich-cutting, filling medicine bottles with milk, and a feverish hunt for bat and ball, without which the expedition was doomed to failure. After my sister and I were washed and combed into passable neatness, we would board a bus in Bethnal Green Road which put us down within walking distance of the Park gates. Here we joined a procession of friends and neighbours going the same way.

At the actual park entrance, the road became a bridge over the canal. We would pause for a moment to look down on the naked boys who bathed in its murky waters. Often, as we watched, a policeman would suddenly appear and give chase, since bathing was strictly prohibited. This invariably added spice to the day's excitement.

Victoria Park was the nearest oasis of any size in our sector of the Mittel East. For many families, it became the substitute for a holiday in the country. A visit to the park meant space for the children to play and rowing boats for hire. For the less energetic, a large motor boat left the landing stage at regular intervals and for the outlay of a penny you chug-chugged a circuit of the several islands that dotted the lake. On the largest of these, a pagoda, painted green, black, red and gold, towered over the willows that lined the banks. It was here that we re-enacted many a Doctor Fu Manchu adventure, accompanied by blood-curdling shrieks and genuine tears, shed by our tortured younger brothers and sisters.

The park also sported a beautiful hothouse full of palm trees, flowers in blossom, and the inevitable aspidistras. It was from this place that all the plants displayed in the parlours of our relatives originated. My father had surreptitiously obtained a cutting on one of our visits.

I loved Victoria Park. For my sister and me, it was a land of adventure and discovery. We would find our uncertain way to the aviary and, with noses pressed against the wire netting, watch the antics of strange and colourful birds that chirped and twittered within. Nearby, a large white cockatoo chained to a precarious perch, would screech and spread its wings.

My parents would walk across the park past the lake, to a grassy patch by a drinking fountain, which looked like the Albert Memorial in minia-ture, steps and all. Here, an old blanket would be spread, and our many parcels of food opened. Soon we were eating sandwiches, platzels and bagels left over from breakfast, and drinking milk from the medicine bottles that, despite incessant rinsings, still added a flavour of paregoric to the contents. My father would then unfold copies of the *Yiddish Express* and the *Amerikaner Zeitung*, hand one to my mother, and they would stretch out comfortably, shoes off, to enjoy an uninterrupted read or sleep.

This was our time to play cricket with the other children. Because my father was a cabinet-maker, I possessed a splendid bat which prerogative ensured for me the first innings at all times. At regular intervals we would run back to our parents for an orange to be peeled and scrupulously shared, or a bar of chocolate. Father would give me a sixpence and my sister and I would rush off madly to the nearby refreshment kiosk for a lemonade and ice cream. This moment was always a high spot in the day's outing. We would feel very grown up seated at the little green tables, luxuriously licking away at our ices served in thick cone-shaped glasses. Here we had our place in the sun, to enjoy the luxury of nature and wide open spaces. The narrow streets and box-like rooms of our overcrowded tenements were forgotten for an hour or two. For my parents, it was a moment to rest from the cares and worries of their daily life. Later, when the sun went down and a chill came off the ground, the blanket was folded up and replaced in my mother's shopping bag; shoes were put on again, and after my sister and I had been combed and our faces flannel-washed at the fountain, we trekked across the park towards the bus stop and home.

During my childhood we visited many other open spaces, but I always preferred Victoria Park. I got to know every inch of it like the back of my hand. You see, it was my park!

The Nut Game

The street was my playground. Here we played football with a small rubber ball, or a rectangular substitute made from sheets of newspaper tightly bound with string. This possessed no bounce whatsoever, but had the advantage of leaving window glass unshattered on impact.

Cricket was also a sport in season. Any lamp-post served as a wicket, but wear and tear on local windows was dreadful to contemplate. We were forced to install a 'policeman watcher' at strategic street corners, who would signal the approach of the Law, with loud cries of 'Here comes a copper!' On hearing this, we would vanish into any open doorway and wait until the 'all clear' was given. To be caught was a doubly painful experience. Having frightened you into revealing your name and address, the policeman would march you home holding your ear as hostage. Mother would be fully informed about the crime, and, anxious to pacify the law, did so by tanning the hide off you on the spot.

We played other games: hop-scotch, gamma (with chunks of stone levered out of the roadway), tip-cat, touch, wallee, diabolo and marbles.

50

It was during the Pesach interlude that real peace descended on the neighbourhood. New shoes and new suits slowed down the vigorous amongst us. Skill displaced brawn, and all was quiet in the land.

★   ★   ★

My mother said 'You shouldn't make the suit dirty, kiss me and close the street door'. It was Pesach 1920. The Great War had come to its bloody end, and the streets in my quarter of Bethnal Green still had vestiges of bunting clinging to lamp-posts, souvenirs of local Peace parties.

I was ten years old, and about to try my luck in the nut-game. Chambord Street was just around the corner. This was the local casino. Within its forty yards of pavement and stone-cobbled roadway a hundred games were under way. It was towards this rendezvous that I hurried, my store of nuts carefully tied up in a white matza-meal bag. I started with the box game. Boot boxes with small square holes cut in each corner and middle of the lids, looking like giant dice, resting five-side up, were for the non-skilled punter. The players stood in the kerb (careful not to rub the patent-leather toe-caps of squeaking new shoes), and attempted to throw nuts into the holes, each of which had a number representing the winning odds. Having expended about ten of my hoard, and showing a small profit, I wandered down the road to try my luck on the marble board.

In principle, this was similar to the shoe box. It was made of wood, and looked like a bridge with five narrow arches cut into it. (It was made at school in the carpenter's shop, following the pencil sharpener exercise). Here the odds were recorded in indelible pencil over each arch. Unlike the box, skill came into operation, You rolled the nuts, taking careful aim before doing so. If you have played bowls, you will appreciate what practice was necessary to overcome the natural bias of a Spanish nut.

Yet another game was 'Odd or Even'. You played this against an opponent by dipping your hand into a bag, and withdrawing an unspecified number of nuts, shouting 'Odd or Even?' If your adversary guessed correctly, he took the fistful: If not, he paid you the same number. This was a game for cissies and girls.

All along the kerbside of both pavements, the bowed backs of boys indicated that 'Hittings and Spannings' was going on. To play this required a steady eye and a good span. You rolled a nut five yards or so along the gutter, and your opponent tried to hit it with his nut. (Specially rounded nuts would fetch as much as ten or fifteen ordinary ones, on the exchange.) If you were hit, you paid over a pre-arranged number of nuts. If he did not hit you, but could span the difference, a smaller reward was offered. Quick wit and good eyesight were essential qualities in this field. For instance, your adversary's nut would be stopped by a matchbox or other obstruction in the kerb. Quick as a flash you shouted 'no moves' and rolled your nut towards the matchbox, which made a hit possible and a span a certainty.

Games would go on for hours. Tears and blows would take their toll of players. Preoccupied adults would walk across a game and crush all the nuts, followed by strings of ripe Jewish curses and counter-threats 'to tell de mudder of you'. It was great fun, and around tea-time the groups would break up for the day, the fortunates with their linen bags bursting with spoils: the losers, with a few dumps (a sort of charity hand-out to those who had lost their all) clutched in their hands. Back home, we would eat our buttered matzas, plava cake and yesterday's lutkas sprinkled with sugar. Afterwards, we would count the nuts and plan tomorrow's coup.

Marriages Were Made in Heaven

Romance was something you read about in books, or it flickered before you on a cinema screen. Soft lights and sweet music came at a premium too high to be met on a workman's wages. Most of the marriages that were solemnised in the local synagogues were invariably the end product of a dozen family meetings conducted on a business basis. Love was a mere side issue—an acceptable bonus on a good investment. From the age of fourteen the natives were forced to work. Money was earned by the sweat of one's brow in tiny overcrowded workshops given over to the production of furniture or clothing. Standards were high but wages low. A good cabinet-maker earned about £2 10s. a week. His hours were 8 a.m. to 8 p.m. which included half an hour's break for lunch and tea. With overtime, this might be raised to £3. Marriage meant sharing an already inadequate income with a wife. The advent of children made the prospect unthinkable. Thus the voice of the marriage broker was heard in the land.

★   ★   ★

One Sunday evening, my mother said to me 'Put on the best suit and clean the shoes. We are going to Auntie Lottie.' Auntie Lottie was my mother's married sister, living in a ground-floor cum-basement of an old house in Spital Square. In its prime, the house had belonged to the gentry. Inside, the walls were of panelled mahogany and an elaborate carved handrail ornamented the magnificent staircase leading to the first floor. When the house was eventually demolished, the staircase was purchased by a museum.

I liked visiting my uncle and aunt. He was a printer by profession and had a wonderful selection of books and magazines which I was permitted to leaf through without the usual fuss and bother meted out to the young.

The large front room on the ground floor was used for entertaining. It was here that female members of our family were introduced to prospective husbands. My aunt, assisted by the girl's mother, would bake yeast cakes, prepare gefilte fish, chop dozens of herrings and butter masses of rye bread, all of which was carefully arranged on a large damask-covered table in the middle of the room. The mantelpiece over the grand fireplace bristled with ornaments, some so large that they had to be tied on to the mirror-shelves for safety. Potted aspidistras were dotted round the room on slender stands made by my father.

Around eight o'clock, the participants would begin to drift in, greeted by my aunt or uncle with a hearty handshake and a glass of whisky or brandy. 'The young lady', perhaps a cousin or daughter of one of my aunt's landsleit, would arrive with full family entourage, their clothes smelling faintly of mothballs. She would probably be wearing her smartest dress with her hair combed into a fashionable bob or shingle. The young man, supported by the Shadchen, was formally introduced and the couple left to exchange a few embarrassed pleasantries. My uncle would join in their conversation and help to ease the tension. From then on it was up to them.

The Shadchen was a professional marriage arranger imported from the Ghettos of Russia and Poland. He travelled from district to district leaving a trail of wedlock in his wake. He was the public relations man of the early 20s and flourished in the Mittel East. Parents of nubile daughters entrusted him with their hopes and aspirations. It was he, like the Assyrians of old, who came down like a benign wolf on the fold of Bachelors of Art or doctors, dangling the dowries before them. He also did a lower-class trade in furriers, tailors and cabinet makers, anxious to settle down and set up homes of their own. The Shadchen made all things possible—on a percentage basis.

Soon the parents of the intended would withdraw into an adjacent room with him and get down to business. If the young man, please God, was willing to plight his troth with their lovely daughter (no evil eye befall her), they would make a nice wedding and help the young couple financially, and so on.

Meanwhile, back in the front room, the air would be thick with cigarette smoke and hearty conversation. Inevitably, a game of solo had been started, and the couple, now seated side by side (a good omen), were joining in the good-natured kibbitzing that was an onlooker's prerogative.

The party eventually broke up around eleven o'clock in an orgy of handshaking, mazeltovs and tearful embraces. We youngsters would undergo a torture of wet kisses and pinched cheeks, administered by loving relatives. Compensation was offered by way of a penny to spend on sweets. The young man, suitably impressed by his grand reception, had already made a date with his intended. All was right with the world, and love would find its way.

The Seaside Beside the Sea

Work was the be-all and end-all for the breadwinner. Without a job, however poorly paid, a man could not survive in the native quarter. In order to keep his wife and family fed and clothed my father spent most of the day in his workshop during the busy season. He left home at dawn and returned, tired and weary, long after we were asleep. To us, his children, he was a nebulous figure who suddenly materialised at our table for the Sabbath dinner, after which he would kiss us fondly and retire to bed. But there was one week of the year during which we became a real family. It was the seven days holiday we spent by the sea. This was only made financially possible by the ingenious skimping and saving effected by my mother. Much of my father's overtime money went into this fund, banked in a large cracked teapot that was kept on the top shelf of the kitchen dresser. When the pot was full it was time to go.

*　　*　　*

A few days before August Bank Holiday my mother said to me, 'Go empty your rubbish from the baskets and bring them into my bedroom'. It was approaching holiday time, and my sister and I were full of excited anticipation. We rushed up and down the stairs running errands for my mother, who was busily engaged in packing the leather-strapped rectangular straw baskets with our clothes. We were going to St Leonards-on-Sea, where a Mrs Davis rented us two bedrooms and use of kitchen.

Soon the great day arrived and we were decked out in our best clothes, my father looking particularly spruce in a trilby hat instead of the sawdust-covered cap he always wore to work. The two-hour journey to the coast passed in a flash, as did the rye bread sandwiches of cream cheese and pickled cucumbers.

On arrival at Warrior Square Station, we boarded an open-top tram to Silverhill, where we alighted and walked the short distance to Mrs Davis's house. She inevitably greeted us at the door, hugging and kissing my mother, sister and me with the unabashed fervour of a close relative.

Inside, the house had an aroma of its own. The fragrance of freshly baked bread and lavender permeated the hallway. For me, this became the moment when our holiday really began. Upstairs we ran to our room, which was next-door to our parents. Everything was clean, bright and sweet. From the window we could see the garden below full of the fruit and vegetables we would eat during the week. On the washstand an ornamental china ewer full of water stood in a matching basin.

My sister and I washed and changed into our holiday clothes, laid out on the beds for us by mother. I wore an open-neck cricket shirt, short grey flannel trousers held up by a snake-buckle elastic belt, coloured in yellow and black horizontal stripes. My sister wore a blouse with a huge sailor collar, a hand pleated skirt of blue serge, white socks and brown rubber plimsolls.

Thus attired, we would join our parents to take a tram ride down the hill for our first sight of the sea, and to renew our acquaintance with the many shop keepers who flourished near the promenade.

During that magic week we bathed every morning, undressing in a house-shaped caravan on huge wheels that was drawn down to the sea's edge by a horse. My mother had a lovely home-made costume which she wore when bathing. It was made of a dark material, had a square neck, a large collar with white piping, and a frilly kneelength skirt. An elasticated mob cap was worn with this ensemble. It was virtually impossible for her to swim in it, as the material became water-logged and dragged her to the bottom.

Most of the women did their bathing clinging to a large rope which ran from shore to sea. With uninhibited shrieks of laughter, they dipped and splashed in the waves that thundered on to the stony shingle.

In a few days, our Mittel East pallor was replaced by a healthy tan. My parents rested on deck chairs. We sent messages on the backs of picture cards, to friends and relatives in the quarter. We visited Alexandria Park and the pumping station where Mrs Davis' husband worked as an engineer. We wandered around nearby Hastings, and watched the leathery-faced fishermen hanging and mending their nets. It was a world full of exciting tarry smells and sturdy boats. I loved it.

It was also during this brief sojourn by the sea that my father reintegrated himself into our lives. We became a completed family unit, enjoying the unaccustomed luxury of taking our daily meals together, going on walks together or just sitting quietly on the beach in a compact group.

The end of our holiday was marked by the purchase of sticks of pink-coated peppermint rock, with the word 'Hastings' running through the middle. When we returned to the Mittel East, these were distributed according to established protocol and gave most of the recipients a nagging toothache. On the Monday following our return home my mother did the holiday laundry. There was always a residue of sand at the bottom of the galvanized washtub. When this was rinsed away our holiday was truly over.

Pastoral Symphony

Flowers did not flourish in my part of the world. The fortunate few whose homes boasted a strip of garden in front or at the rear of the premises, worked like navvies to keep a few blooms alive. All this despite the soot and cats of Bethnal Green. Occasionally a geranium would burst into colour and all the neighbours would stand and look at it with pride. The desire for a bit of nature about the place manifested itself in ornamental potted aspidistras, long-stemmed spikey-splayed palm fronds in tubs, and curtains of Virginia creeper on the splintery wood fences that separated one stony backyard from its neighbour. The younger and more adventurous natives of the quarter got away from it all in the green fields of Surrey or Kent. In those days the railway companies were kindly disposed towards the day tripper. For the sum of a shilling and sixpence they would take you there and bring you back. Rambling Clubs and Societies sprang up all over the Mittel East like mushrooms in a forest. They attracted many members, and Sunday after Sunday the approach to London Bridge Station would be crowded with teenage hikers ready to follow their leaders into the great unknown.

* * *

My mother said to me: 'Take the mackintosh on the ramble, it will maybe rain.'

So I added a heavy raincoat to the burden in my haversack. My mother had got up early that Sunday morning to make sandwiches for me as I was going on a club ramble to Leatherhead in Surrey. My friends had agreed to meet under Findlaters Clock by London Bridge and it was towards this rendezvous that I made my way.

On arrival it was difficult to sort out my group. Almost every able-bodied teenager in the Mittel East was off on a trek in Surrey and had arranged to meet under Findlaters Clock. Eventually we sorted ourselves out into the correct parties, and having ascertained that we were all present and correct, wandered off to the booking office for our cheap day return tickets. Our fares seldom rose above the one and sixpenny mark. A two-bob journey took too much time and covered a great deal of territory.

We were a motley crew in our hiking equipage. Good stout shoes, walking sticks (available at any junk shop for about threepence), rucksacks and brown paper parcels giving off tantalising odours of fresh brown bread (with seeds), fried egg, smoked salmon (an heiress, this girl), and the astringent smell of oranges covered us like a cloud. The men, for the most part, wore plus-fours and sports jackets. A dashing trilby or two broke the monotony of curly locks and shingled napes. The girls orna-mented the occasion with colourful dresses in summer and bright hand-knitted jumpers in the evening. The more fashion-conscious covered their shingled heads and most of their faces with cloche hats.

Tickets in hands, we negotiated the barrier and boarded the waiting train. A struggle always ensued to seat oneself near a pretty girl or, taking a long and more materialistic view, one who was known to carry out-of-the-run-of-the-mill sandwiches. The stringy luggage racks were soon loaded with our gear, and we would settle down comfortably for the hour's journey.

Time passed quickly in good-natured banter and community singing. Somebody always produced a students' song book, and week after week we would sing our favourites as if for the first time. On arrival at our destination we detrained and, according to sex, disappeared into the Ladies or Gentlemen, just to be on the safe side. Much relieved by this timely intermission the group assembled outside the station where our leader, map in hand, looking like Columbus about to discover America, gave us a briefing on where and how we were going.

Soon we were under way. Leafy lanes, sun-drenched fields, birds singing, and above all, the perfume of good clean unadulterated air surrounded us. We sauntered along ancient Roman paths, through woods and meadow-land, singing and laughing, with all the outward appearance of carefree youth, except that none of us was carefree. Many miles later, by an ancient churchyard, a halt was called for lunch. Came a busy time for opening rucksacks, untying parcels, offers to swap egg sandwiches for chicken or wurst for salad. Cameras were brought into action, and many a married woman today still treasures in her bottom drawer the slowly fading snapshots of old boy friends taken on these light-hearted outings. Then, in the welcome shade of near-by trees, the lovers and their lasses exchanged secrets, whilst the tough unattached types smoked their pipes and smiled in faint derision. Other members of the group would make pillows out of their rucksacks and settle down for an hour's tanning in the sun. In the distance we could hear the traffic going by on the Dorking/Leatherhead Road, but here by the ancient church was peace and quiet.

Rested and fed, we resumed our itinerary. The next step was tea. This had been arranged a week before by the advance party, consisting of our appointed leader and one committee-man or woman. Expenses involved were covered by a special fund to which all members of the club contributed. We had a six-mile uphill walk ahead in a blazing sun towards the little farm where our tea had been booked. The higher we climbed, the more magnificent the view that spread itself below us. Finally, at the very top of the rise, the farm came into view and was greeted by a very hearty and thankful cheer from our party.

The tea was always magnificent, and averaged about a shilling a head. For this you were provided with bread and butter, and jam, ad lib, home-made cakes, scones, lettuce, tomatoes, cucumber, watercress, and all the tea you could drink. It also included towels and soap for a wash and brush-up on arrival.

With tea over, it was now time for home. In the gathering dusk, arms would steal round waists as couples paired off and sauntered towards the station. A scramble for seats in the train, and it was farewell Leather-head and heigho the Mittel East. Tired but happy, we would reach home and sleep the sleep of the just, having covered about twenty-five miles in our day's outing.

Shopping at Mrs Rubin's

Shopping was no problem. Scarcely a street existed without its attendant shops catering for the immediate needs of the quarter. Food in all its infinite variety was readily available. The only hindrance was lack of money with which to make the purchase. This was a disease which flourished in the Mittel East and spread unchecked to its environs. Families had to be fed so the shopkeepers allowed credit. No leather-bound ledger recorded the purchase. With the stub of a carpenter's pencil licked between words, the grocer would laboriously scrawl huge figures on a white crimped-edged bag. This was handed to the customer after the same total was recorded on a blue sugarbag, which the grocer retained. On father's payday we did the rounds of the shops paying our debts. In addition to the shops proper, sundry barrowmen trundled their wheelbarrows through the streets crying their wares in Yiddish; this trade was strictly cash. To eke out a minimal livelihood meant pushing their barrows over miles of cobbled roadway in all weathers. Many of these itinerant

EGGS

traders later established chains of foodshops which are still flourishing today.

★   ★   ★

Sometimes when I was reading the *Magnet* or *Gem* my mother would say to me; 'Go now to Mrs Rubin and buy for me a few things for supper tonight'. Reluctantly I would leave Harry Wharton or Bob Cherry, put on my Eton cap with its gold-braided school badge and go off on my errand. The shopping list, written on the margin of a piece of newspaper in my mother's meticulous Yiddish, was clutched in my hand. I would run along Gibraltar Walk, turn left at the corner pub, and then down Virginia Road, where Mrs Rubin's grocery was about 50 yards along the right-hand side of the street. You could smell it at 30 feet away. Schmaltz-herring, pickled cucumbers, black olives, roll-mops with onions, kippers, bloaters and an all-embracing aroma of freshly ground coffee spread their tantalising odours, like the gravy lines in the Bisto advertisement.

Inside, the shop was cluttered up like a nightmare. Tin boxes of biscuits were stacked around the walls from floor to ceiling; crates of eggs were everywhere. On the marbletop counter, jagged blocks of Dutch butter, complete with wooden patters, shared the limited space with kippers, bloaters, smoked herring, and an elaborate device for grinding coffee beans. Pride of place was given to a side of smoked salmon, resplendent on its horizontal board and flanked by a long slender razor-sharp knife.

Mrs Rubin was a tiny, chubby, button-nosed woman who invariably wore a knitted hat, like a lumberjack's, and a voluminous fat-stained blue overall. The shop was usually full of chattering women whose kiddies ran amok among the boxes. Attempts to fall head-first into herring barrels or pull down the precariously stacked sharp-edged biscuit boxes were stalled off by streams of angry Yiddish and a few sharp slaps around the face. The children's crying scarcely dented the conversational barrier.

Being about eleven years old at the time put me into a near-adult category in Mrs Rubin's estimation. On catching sight of me waiting patiently behind her vociferous clientele, she would lean across the counter between the Dutch butter and a glass tank full of pickled cucumbers to give me a handful of broken biscuits that always tasted faintly of smoked salmon. To this day, whenever I eat a broken biscuit the ghost of a far-off smoked salmon hovers around me like an ectoplasm.

One by one, the women would collect their groceries until it was my turn to be served. I would hand over the order to Mrs Rubin, who would mutter each item out loud in Yiddish as she reached out for it. My greatest joy was to be permitted to use the coffee-grinding machine. The beans and a chunk of chicory were put into the angular funnel on top of the contraption and I would turn the giant wheel by its enormous handle until the tin box under the chute was full of ground aromatic coffee.

When my order was completed, Mrs Rubin would wipe off part of the counter with her apron, take a stubby carpenter's pencil from some mysterious recess in her cash drawer and laboriously record my purchases on a blue sugar bag which she impaled on a spike hanging from a shelf behind her. She then wrapped up the bits and pieces of my order in a sheet of the *Jewish Express*, pinched my cheeks with her smoked-salmony fingers and said 'Give my regards to the mother'. Reluctantly I would leave the gloomy interior buoyed up by the knowledge that I could nibble a taster or two from the package in my hand on the way home.

Measure for Measure

Clothes were bought with care and due regard for durability. Fortunate indeed was the family which, by luck rather than judgment, had so produced their children that the clothing outgrown by one of them could be handed down to his or her junior. This meant a considerable saving in money. It also created the necessity for buying good quality clothing in the first place. Practically every boy, from his barmitzvah suit onwards, was taken to the tailor every two or three years depending on his rate of growth, for a made-to-measure suit. This was a must. Ready-to-wear was a nasty phrase in the Yiddish vocabulary, something no self-respecting parents would countenance. You bought your own cloth and had it made up by the tailor. Almost everyone in the quarter had a landsman or relative who was a tailor. In tiny, overcrowded, ill-lit dwelling places converted into workshops some of the finest tailors in the land plied their craft. The man who made little Moishe's first suit probably produced Lord Derby's morning coat. Today, the private tailor, like good manners, is practically a thing of the past. His warm, friendly almost-one-of-the-family presence has been replaced by a commission man in a soulless chain-store.

★ ★ ★

One Sunday morning before Pesach, my mother said to me: 'Go put on the overcoat. We are going to the Lane to buy cloth for a new suit.'

68

I was fouteen years old at the time. Until then, in order to save money, my mother, who was an expert dressmaker, used to make all my clothes. This included vests (the best flannel), shirts and suits with a Peter Pan collar. She also knitted my socks, gloves and scarves. It was after my barmitzvah that the decision was made to put me into long trousers. Hitherto I had gone around in knickerbockers, but my rapid growth made me a rather incongruous figure.

'It must be made by the tailor', my father said, 'we will go to cousin Oreh.'

Oreh lived in the West End and was a high-class tailor making special orders for firms like Harrods.

The first stage in the suit saga was the purchase of suitable cloth in the Lane. My parents had a landsman in the woollens' business who would sell us material at wholesale prices. We departed on our pilgrimage to the market place where the shop was situated. Inside it was dismally dark, and even during the day a solitary gas light did little to brighten the atmosphere. Large bolts of cheviots, worsteds, tweeds, serge and flannel were stacked all over the place. My father's friend came out of the shop-parlour to greet us and said what a big boy I was getting, no evil eye befall you.

'We want a piece of cloth for the boy for a suit', my mother said. 'Maybe you got a nice blue serge, but should be heavy.'

By some uncanny instinct, the cloth was immediately found and produced. We all walked out into the street to examine its colour by daylight. Being Sunday morning, the pavements were crowded with shoppers, so we edged our way into the crowd and scrutinised the material. My dad liked it: my mother approved the weight and quality and said to me in a voice that brooked no contradiction, 'this is what you will have'. Back we trooped inside. The material was measured off against a brass yardstick screwed on to the dark mahogany counter, cut with tailor's shears and wrapped in a Yiddish newspaper. My father paid and shook hands with his friend. My mother shook hands with him. I shook hands with him. He pinched my cheek and said 'What a big boy he's getting, no evil eye befall him.'

The following Sunday afternoon we went to Liverpool Street Station and boarded an Inner Circle train to Euston Square. My father's cousin lived within twenty minutes' walk from this station. We arrived and were given a boisterous welcome by Oreh and his family. Tea was soon served, and we set to with a will. The dining room was in the basement and it had obviously been the servants' kitchen when the house was in its prime. The only natural light filtered through a large iron grating that was at pavement level.

The workshop was on the ground floor. Tea over, we all trooped upstairs for something everybody referred to as 'the measure'. Oreh, jacket off and tape measure round his neck, produced notebook and pencil and began to 'measure me up'. Chest, shoulder width, inside arm, outside arm, waist, seat, outside leg, inside leg, all were carefully recorded in his notebook, together with some strange hieroglyphics that conveyed certain details to Oreh when he was cutting the cloth.

The workshop fascinated me. Large cardboard and brown paper patterns hung from hooks on the wall, interspersed with prints of elegantly moustached gentlemen wearing beautifully tailored suits. The work tables were chest-high against me and were littered with baisted garments in various stages of make-up. Huge pairs of shears and boxes of tailor's chalk were ready to hand. In the fireplace a gas stove housed several enormous irons which were used for pressing seams and finished work.

The measuring completed to Oreh's satisfaction, an appointment was made for the first 'try-on'. A fortnight later I found myself back in the workshop, draped in a piece of serge that vaguely resembled a suit. The jacket sported but one sleeve and the trousers had no visible means of support. I was asked to turn around and was scrutinised from every angle. Each critical remark made by my parents was followed by bits of my suit being speared with pins or wildly drawn upon with chalk. The solitary sleeve was ripped out and repinned in a new position. The canvas lapels were trimmed with the shears, and the turn-ups of my trousers adjusted in accordance with my mother's wishes. All this was obviously normal procedure for Oreh. He did what he had to do without any display of ill temper or a cross word. After half-an-hour of absolute agony for me, Oreh stopped tearing, stitching, cutting and chalking, took off his tape-measure, said 'Is now good', and told me to get dressed.

A week before Pesach, the suit was completed. It arrived carefully folded and padded with tissue paper. When I put it on, everybody said: 'I wish you well to wear it'. On the second day of Yomtov, I discovered a sixpence in my trouser pocket. For good luck, from cousin Oreh, my mother told me.

Workers' Praytime

Most of the inhabitants of the Mittel East left the land of their birth under pressure of poverty or pogrom, taking with them a minimum of clothing, bedding, cooking utensils and a deep-rooted belief in the God of their fathers. The quarter offered them a respite from persecution and an opportunity to eke out a livelihood of sorts. Cabinet-makers, furriers and tailors joined their brethren in the ill-lit, badly ventilated sweatshops set up by earlier immigrants, where for six days of the week they worked to earn their bread and rent. But the seventh day was sacred, set aside for rest and prayer. Any room large enough to hold ten men or more was established as a synagogue. No becostumed cantor called the faithful to prayer: no officious shamus bestowed the weekly mitzvahs. Here the Spirit was all. It was in the home of my great uncle, in a dingy cobble-stoned street in Bethnal Green, that I first put on a prayer shawl, as a yet unbarmitzvahed member of a congregation.

*　　*　　*

One Friday night, my mother said to me, 'Tomorrow, please God, you will go to shool by Uncle Charlie.'

Uncle Charlie was my great uncle who lived about fifteen minutes walk from our home. He was a huge broad-shouldered man, and the father of five sons and one daughter. Like my father he was a cabinet-maker, working in a shack at the far end of the scrubby garden adjoining his house. He wore steel-rimmed spectacles, and had a long square-cut beard like the rabbi in Rembrandt's painting. It was in his home that my mother, as a fifteen-year-old immigrant from Lida, lived until she met and married my father. Because of his large family, Uncle Charlie rented a complete house. The front room, ground floor, was used as a synagogue on the Sabbath. A portable, beautifully made wardrobe served as an Ark for the solitary Scroll it housed. On a shelf beneath it, the prayer books and Pentateuchs were stored, so that the sin of carrying on the Sabbath could be avoided.

Every Saturday, without exception, at least fourteen men would assemble for the Service, Uncle Charlie providing five of them as well as leading the prayers. Being the only child present, by virtue of my relationship with Uncle Charlie, I was unmercifully spoiled by the attentions of my fellow congregants. Clothed in a tiny tallis, blue silk yarmelke on my curly hair, I must have looked like the infant Samuel, but in knickerbockers instead of a nightshirt.

The service itself was simple. Uncle Charlie stood at a high desk facing the Ark, and in the traditional sing-song voice, led us through the intricacies of the Sabbath prayers. I was about ten years old at the time and Hebrew presented no difficulties, so I joined in the reading with enthusiasm, earning an endearing pinch on the cheek from my proud father and the snuffy fingers of his friends.

Before the concluding prayers, and following the reading of the weekly portion of the Torah, an impromptu sermon would be delivered by a visiting learned man. This was invariably in Yiddish besprinkled with Hebrew quotations and English grace notes. My favourite speaker was known to us all as Meshuginer Moishe. He was a sincere and impassioned orator who brooked not a hair-breadth departure from the Holy Law. Clothed in a huge tallis that kept slipping off his shoulders with every sweep of his hand, at the same time giving off an overpowering odour of mothballs, Moishe would face the congregants, take aim and fire his opening quotation. Before the shock had subsided, Moishe was under way. He would pick his quotation clean to the bone, flavouring it with Gemorah and Mishna spices, before offering it for final consumption.

To look at, he was a Messianic figure; wild, staring eyes behind wire-rimmed spectacles; a long pure white beard and moustache that he tugged between spasms of tallis hitching. At his best he could go on for hours without repeating himself. After half an hour's onslaught, the listeners would cry out, 'It's enough, Moishe—it's already enough.' Moishe would stop in mid-sentence, lift his tallis back in position, raise his spectacles onto his high wrinkled forehead, adjust his almost-off yarmelke, and look wildly round at his audience.

It was at this stage that Moishe became the Meshuginer. He would begin to berate the congregation (with quotations, of course) for their

lack of Yiddishkeit, their lack of learning, their lack of respect, until
Uncle Charlie, who knew him of old, would put his arm round his
shoulders and lead him quietly back to his seat. The service would then
continue, Moishe's anger frittering itself away in the sharpness of his
responses. After the final hymn, he was placated by being invited to make
the Kiddush. The men had their whisky; I was given wine, buttered
brown bread with sliced schmaltz herring and a huge slice of ginger cake.
Afterwards, we shook hands all round and wished each other 'Good
Shabbas'.

As we left Uncle Charlie's for home we could hear Moishe starting up
another row. My father would look at me, smile and say, 'That Moishe,
bless him; is he a meshuginer!'.

Beggar's Opera

One of the major side effects of the perennial poverty in which we lived, was the horde of professional schnorrers or beggars who wandered through the sidestreets of the native quarter soliciting alms. Like a plague of locust they would descend on the soft-hearted inhabitants and feast on whatever a hard luck story or a 'nebach' expression could produce. The aftermath of the recent Great War contributed to this sad state of affairs, introducing a touch of originality by way of amputees on a platform trolley or swinging on crutches, their chests clinking with medals. Apart from the straight cadgers who worked the district, there were the talented buskers who sang or played for their supper, investing their meagre earnings in pints of mild and bitter readily obtainable in the street-corner pubs. Finally, in a class of their own were the synagogue beadles cum weekly subscription collectors, who carried a remunerative if illicit side line in the sale of wines and spirits, or the more legitimate purveying of religious texts and flannel underwear.

★　　★　　★

'Take a penny from mine purse on the dresser and give it to Reb Chaim downstairs by the street door,' said my mother to me. It was Sunday morning in the native quarter and thanks to redecoration of the premises my Hebrew class was closed for a week whilst painting was in progress; hence my being home at the time. 'Reb Chaim,' as we called him, was a dedicated schnorrer who had served his apprenticeship in some foreign stiebel, and had graduated with honours. His stock-in-trade was a leather-bound book of religious quotations printed in 6 point Hebrew/Yiddish, one of which he would cut out with a pair of nail scissors attached to his coat lapel by a piece of string.

My mother was a regular customer as were many of our neighbours. For one penny he would carefully cut out a quotation which was taken at random from the book, so that some of the pages remained fairly intact whilst others resembled the fringe of a shawl. If you gave him a halfpenny, the quotation would be suitably devalued. The actual wording on these cuttings was similar to those found in Christmas crackers and were mainly clichés, but like the prognostications of the gypsy fortune tellers who roamed the streets, were taken rather seriously. My mother would read the tiny slip of paper out loud, and immediately relate the message to some proposed family action under contemplation. The slips were stored in an empty Van Houten's cocoa tin, and the contents consulted from time to time like a witch doctor seeking an augury in the entrails of a sheep.

Beggars in many guises wandered through the quarter, including the ubiquitous barrel-organ players who jangled away almost daily, their catchy rhythms inducing the little girls to dance together in instinctive ballet movements. If the repertoire was to the listener's liking, halfpennies and pennies would rain down from the windows of the surrounding tenements.

We were also visited by a couple of cornet players who were Friday afternoon regulars, that being the recognised pay day for the workers. They played facing each other on either side of the road. My favourite tune was 'Santa Lucia', which was their signing off number. They would walk into the two local pubs holding out an open leather pouch into which pennies were dropped by the patrons. The landlord usually offered them a pint in lieu of money.

Another regular was the harmonium and spoons duo. They usually followed the cornet players. With feet peddling like mad to raise the wind to play his mini-organ, the performer would break into a lively tempo accompanied by his partner on the spoons. Keeping in perfect rhythm, the spoons would be tapped on everything in sight by their bowler-hatted unsmiling manipulator. Up and down his arm, on the head and shoulders of the harmonium man, on the back of a stray dog who yelped away in fright, up and down the legs of the children, who, fascinated by his skill; always came to watch him play.

After the Great War, the procession of itinerant beggars increased. Pathetic creatures on crutches, or with pinned up empty sleeves, passed through the quarter offering nothing but their deformities in exchange for the pennies they immediately spent in the public bar of the local pub.

Then there were the genuine pedlars tramping from door to door, from street to street, with their trays of laces, bachelor buttons, reels of cotton, ribbons and elastic, suspended from their necks by webbing belts. Known by name to most of the housewives, they managed to eke out a meagre livelihood in halfpenny and penny sales.

A popular hawker in the quarter was 'Bugs & Fleas' Moishe. His stock consisted entirely of home-made toffee. Coconut, hazelnut, monkey nut, figs and raisins, and slabs of teeth-aching treacle toffee poured onto marble slabs and sold by the ha'porth. 'Bugs & Fleas' was a great favourite, his nickname stemming from the fig and raisin toffee which looked like a plastic flypaper. A halfpenny bought you two ounces, and a certain visit to the nearest Dental Clinic as a bonus. Moishe was a splendid looking man, nearly six feet tall and sporting a magnificent bushy beard. He was always immaculately clean and wore a snow-white carpenter's apron over his normal clothes. If you did not have the cash to buy anything, Moishe would always give you a piece of 'Bugs & Fleas' as a free 'taster'.

It's Cheaper in the Lane

Threaded through the native quarter like the main arteries of the human body were the markets where the staples of life, spread out on rickety stalls, were offered to the casual passer-by. It was here that the natives haggled for their purchases of fruit, fish, vegetables, poultry and clothing. Here also the itinerant quack with the gift of the gab separated his gullible victims from their hard-earned money in exchange for specifics that cured everything from piles to pimples. The cries of the vendors, the chatter of the shoppers and the sickly sweet smell of rotting vegetation, acted as a homing beacon for the natives, who with baskets at the ready filtered into the hurly-burly to become part of it. It was here that neighbour encountered neighbour to exchange news and gossip as they toured the stalls in search of bargains. Unlike the local shops where credit was accepted, market transactions were strictly cash. Marked up prices were merely the basis for argument, a challenge to the canny shopper who knew from experience that every purchase carried with it the moral obligation to haggle. The air would become thick with the thrust and counterthrust of pleading, invective, denigration or downright insult, until the seller admitted defeat and reduced the asking price by a penny or two. Flushed with victory, the shopper would gird up her loins for the next assault. Going to market was a daily chore for the housewife in the Mittel East. Foodstuffs could not be kept too long in the inadequate larders provided by the landlords.

*   *   *

'I am going to the Lane, now', said my mother to me one Sunday morning. 'You want to come with?'

Our nearest market was in Brick Lane, a turning off the main Bethnal Green Road and extended to the railway arch near Hare Street, into which it overflowed. I loved wandering between the crowded stalls, listening to the costers crying out their wares. My mother with a large basket over her arm, black leather concertina purse firmly gripped in her hand, would launch herself into the fray, like a stately liner sliding down the slipway into the sea with me in her wake as a tug boat. She would pause from time to time to squeeze an orange, smell an apple, or handle a cabbage, shake her head, mutter 'Rubbish' and move on to the next stall.

Inevitably we would encounter a neighbour who would stop for a chat with my mother, a circumstance I always welcomed since it left me to my own devices for a while. I would make an immediate bee-line for the stall in front of Waterman's, the kosher butcher, where live eels were kept in a shallow zinc bath in which they wriggled and slithered over each other, unmindful of what fate had in store for them. At a customer's request, the fishmonger would grasp a wriggling handful and throw it into the scale pan for weighing. Then, one by one, he would decapitate, degut and chop them into inch lengths with a long razor-sharp knife. The pieces would continue to move and wriggle despite their irrevocable execution. Fascinated, I would stand and watch the spectacle, repeated time and time again, like an Ancient Roman at the gladiators' circus.

Meanwhile my mother, conversation finished, had already made the first of her several purchases. 'I bought potatoes from the goy by Haltrechts. Such a price he asked me, but I bated him the gonef. Now I'm getting a piece of haddock for supper'. She would wander off to the Hare Street end of the Lane where her regular fishmonger had his pitch. Taking advantage of the good mood engendered by her victory in the potato deal, I obtained permission to continue my solitary ramble round the market.

Along Hare Street, between the stalls, I saw a Negro who had gathered a sizeable audience and a willing victim on whom to demonstrate his magic tooth powder. The volunteer, with a towel tucked round him like a barber's sheet, stood waiting for treatment. After declaiming the wonderful properties of his 'Bubajuba' tooth powder, the negro proceeded to clean his model's teeth vigorously, giving a running commentary on the operation for the benefit of the spectators. I soon found this boring, but the resultant dental gleam cleared the negro's stock of boxes.

Another nearby favourite stop was the Corn Cure King. He would come provided with a suitable patient, usually a whiskery old man, who was seated on a chair with his bare foot raised and resting on a towel spread across the stall. Adjacent to his gnarled foot, as if ready for some major surgical operation, were a set of steel scalpels and tweezers. The 'King' usually wore a white jacket which hinted at the medical nature of his product. He would unleash a flood of sales patter condemning the cutting of corns with knives or razors. Using the scalpels as visual aids, he would brandish them dangerously near the old man's foot and suddenly throw them back on to the towel. Silently he would open a pot of salve and smear it over the hard pad on the model's sole. Then, dramatically, he would take a pair of tweezers and with a flourish, remove the hard skin and hold it aloft for all to see. The audience could hardly wait to buy the salve the Corn King offered them. Further down the road there was another pitch I never failed to visit. It belonged to a watchmaker who did repairs on the spot. Oblivious of the bustle around him, magnifying glass in eye, he calmly operated on sick watches with skill and delicacy. Apart from a box holding his instruments, there was another partitioned off into rows of assorted watch glasses. Near this was a piece of green baize covered with steel-rimmed second-hand spectacles and pince-nez. There were always people trying them on for size and sight. When suited, they were available at a shilling a pair. Sometimes when he was not too busy the watchmaker would let me look through his glass and explain what he was about to replace and why it was necessary.

Returning to Brick Lane I would catch a glimpse of my mother still intent on her buying mission. Finally she would call on me to carry her basket, which was bulging with potatoes, oranges and apples for the guest fruit bowl, cooking apples, a packet of Sabbath candles, a bunch of bananas for slicing into our breakfast sour milk, and the haddock giving off its fishy smell.

As we passed the Lane end of Bacon Street I could hear dice rattling. This indicated an illicit game of Crown and Anchor was in progress.

Punters would be gambling their sixpences on their fancy, whilst a lookout man kept his weather eye open for coppers. At the first warning of the law's approach, the board would be cleared of stake money and closed up to resemble the roof of a large doll's house on which it rested. This was then mock auctioned until the policeman moved off and the interrupted game could continue.

When mother finished her shopping, she would say 'Enough for now We will go home'. Reluctantly I would retrace my footsteps past the still busy stalls, avoiding splintered crates and squashed fruit that littered the road and pavements. Under the fishmonger's barrow the neighbourhood's stray cats were feasting on the entrails thrown there after filleting. By now the eel stall would have sold out, the live fish being replaced by basins of jellied eels and chunks of bread on a plate. There were plenty of customers eating them prior to visiting the public house on the corner.

The babble of Cockney sales patter would go on until one o'clock. On weekdays it would continue into the night, when the stalls were lit up by hissing naphtha flares suspended from the overhead cross-batons on which tarpaulins were spread during wet weather. Like swimmers against the current we pushed our way through the crowd, mother pausing from time to time to exchange pleasantries with friends en route. Eventually we would reach the main road and continue our journey home, with me manfully carrying the now very heavy basket which, when unloaded, would be ready for another trip to the Lane.

Teething Troubles

The native young first encountered the dentist as a direct result of prolonged indulgence in ha'porths of sticky toffee and the endless consumption of sugar-iced buns. The depredation to teeth wrought by these confections failed to respond to the daily counter attack by use of Calvert's Carbolic toothpowder and penultimately erupted into spasms of searing pain that stabbed away sleep and turned the waking hours into a living purgatory. If the application of heated salt in an old sock to the face, a time-honoured remedy against toothache, proved futile, a visit to the dentist would be arranged.

Each family had their favourite practitioner who, besides enjoying their loyal patronage, was also able to communicate with the patient in the language of the country of his or her origin. My parents entrusted the care of their teeth to a Russian lady, whose tiny claustrophobic surgery was tucked away on the first floor above Straker's stationery shop at the Whitechapel end of Osborn Street. Apart from its professional use, the dentist also utilised the same premises as living accommodation so that the windows were constantly draped by lace net and heavy velvet curtains that reduced the brightest outdoor sunlight to a filtered glimmer within. A hissing incandescent gas chandelier was kept permanently lit over the operational area. Dark red flock wall-paper covered most of the walls and was practically obscured at eye-level by dozens of family photographs that seemed to watch one's every move with unsmiling intensity.

The drill with which the dentist ground away decay looked like the spinning wheel in the Sleeping Beauty pantomime on which the unfortunate princess pricks her finger prior to falling into permanent slumber. Its grinding noise became one of my recurrent nightmare sounds, accompanied by the visual image of the lady dentist furiously working the treadle with her foot that peek-a-booed out from under the tent-like cover of her down-to-the-floor skirt.

The coming of school age exposed the innocent young to regular medical and dental care. Periodically, a section of the school assembly hall would be curtained off and class by class, child by child accompanied by a responsible adult, usually mother, would go through an opening in the arras, where stripped to the waist, each child was examined by the visiting doctor. He would tap, prod, and listen through his stethoscope and finally peer into one's mouth in search of teeth requiring treatment. All his findings would be recorded on a medical card by Miss Chick, our teacher, who acted as a nurse substitute during the examination sessions. In time a notice would be forthcoming, informing one's parent that their beloved child was due for treatment at the Dental Clinic.

Our particular rendezvous was in a large converted Georgian house in Hackney Road immediately next door the Queen Mary's Hospital for Children. It was here that my mother took me one memorable afternoon. Inside there were other mums and other children unnaturally spruced up for the occasion that gave the waiting room a festive air. This was confirmed by a huge rocking horse provided by the council on which four children were already jogging up their lunch. In between unaccountable visits to the lavatory we rocked to and fro, activated by a growing fear of the 'upstairs' from which muffled screams filtered into the waiting room below. Several children began to cry and even wet themselves. One by one we were taken upstairs by a nurse who called our names from the medical cards in her hand. Soon it was my turn to go. Years later I saw a film based on Dickens's *Tale of Two Cities* in which an aristocrat leaves the tumbril and bravely mounts the steps leading to the guillotine. It was in a similar frame of mind that I climbed the stairs, dragged by the nurse who sensed both my fear and lack of enthusiasm for the project ahead.

I was ushered into the surgery which apart from a strange looking chair in the centre of the room, was denuded of all furniture. I was eased into this chair and told to 'open wide'. The dentist, a huge man in a white jacket, put a carbolic tasting instrument in my mouth and muttered a few unintelligible remarks to the nurse who came forward and gripped my head between her hands. Like a stage magician producing a rabbit from a hat, a pair of gleaming forceps materialised in the dentist's hand and before I could recover from the sight of it, he extracted three of my teeth. At each wrench I screamed like a banshee and bled into a dark blue jar the perfidious nurse held in front of me. I sobbed bitterly all the way down the stairs and all the way back home. It was only when we reached our flat that I realised I had wet my trousers into the bargain.

Subsequently my experience became a talking point in Standard Three and the gaps in my mouth could be examined by the curious in exchange for a few marbles or half a dozen cigarette cards. It was at this stage of my life that I learned that it profited a man nothing if he gained the world and lost his teeth.

Live and Learn

The majority of the natives in our quarter came from countries where education was the prerogative of the rich or ruling classes. Debarred from the enjoyment of this privilege by discrimination or a total absence of local schools, many of them did manage to learn the language of their mother country as well as Yiddish. Their children, born into the comparative freedom of the native quarter, were given opportunities undreamed of in the distant land of pogroms and anti-semitism.

In sooty red-brick institutions erected at the turn of the century by well-meaning but unimaginative architects, the young were initiated into the mysteries of literature and science by teachers quick to punish and slow to praise. Despite this, many of the young ones in time, entered the major universities via the few scholarships made available to them at the foundation schools. For this opportunity, the senior citizens were prepared to endure economic privation. The unbounded joy of having a potential doctor or teacher in the family made the loss of the few shillings he would contribute to the exchequer as a cabinet-maker or tailor, a sacrifice worth making.

★ ★ ★

'You can go out with Norman when the homework is finished', said my mother to me. Every day, apart from the Sabbath, I was beset by an

overwhelming mass of homework. Literature, maths, physics, history, geography, and the accented irregularities of the French language, all took toll of my personal freedom, gnawing at my enthusiasm like a rat at a wedge of cheese. The carefree cries of my cabinet-maker-to-be-friends heard coming up from the streets below would make the pen grow heavy in my ink-stained fingers, and I would stare out of the window at the vista of chimney pots, overcome with envy and soul-searing frustration.

We lived in a three-roomed flat on the second floor of a terraced house in Gibraltar Walk. The front room, overlooking the street below, was my parents' bedroom. A step away along the passage was the bedroom I shared with my sister. A heavy curtain divided the room so that some sort of privacy could be maintained and give us both the illusion of having a room of our own. Since no other place was available, I did my home-work on the kitchen table sharing the chessboard-patterned oilcloth cover with a large aspidistra in an art-nouveau pot. In moments of abstraction I would stare through its leaves like a tiger in Rousseau's painting, stalking its prey.

The room was tiny and crammed with essential furniture. In one corner a sink jutted out of the wall, two brass taps above it supplying water for our drinking and daily ablutions. It was here that we took turns every morning to wash and father to shave with his cut-throat razor. It was also here that mother peeled and prepared vegetables for our evening meal.

Diagonally opposite, under a small curtained window that let into the room the only uninterrupted daylight, was mother's foot-treadle Singer sewing machine that always reeked of oil. It was here that she spent her few spare moments sewing dresses, shirts and underwear for the family. There was always a bundle of ready-pinned and baisted garments waiting to be stitched together.

At the left of this window and practically invisible in the gloom, was a sofa covered in black American-cloth that shone like a sweating negro and rivalled the Nubian gleam of the Zebra-polished ironwork of the fireplace facing the sink. Winter and summer there was always a fire burning in the grate, a large, once-white enamel kettle on the hob, which supplied the hot water for both tea and washing the 'smalls'. A mesh fender surround kept flying sparks in check and was also used to dry or air laundry. After wash-days the fire would be completely hidden by steaming vests, long pants and pillow cases. Only the sound of the kettle

lid rattling in the steam pressure betrayed its fiery existence. The one decorative note in the room, apart from the flowered wallpaper that covered three of the walls, was the bobble-edged scalloped green plush curtains that hung down from the overmantel above the fireplace.

Dominating the room was a built-in pinewood dresser with drawers and storage cupboards at its base. Here all the family china was on constant display, and ranged from the delicate porcelain cups and saucers, only used when guests were expected, to the coarse every-day ware that showed a chip or two round the edges. From the centre of the ceiling a gaspipe supporting a globe-protected incandescent mantle hung down over my head like the sword of Damocles. When lit at night, the light would burn with a sibilant sigh interrupted by occasional hiccoughs which made a strange popping noise. The gas which fed all the lights and a stove in the passage was recorded on a meter under the sink. The meter lived on the pennies we dropped into its slit-like mouth and was regarded as a potential enemy. It was in this room that I prepared my homework each evening, watched over by my mother in between her immediate domestic chores. Whenever my attention strayed, mother would bring me back to earth by an abrupt command to 'Do the homework!' I would reluctantly abandon my daydreams and return to my text books and enter the gathered facts into the exercise books provided.

Despite the pressing calls on my mother's time she never failed to 'sit-in' on my study periods, such was her determination that I should one day become a college boy. As I grew older the demands on my learning grew greater, more and more extra-curricular work being set by my teachers. The books I had were not always able to supply the information I sought in them. This meant a visit to the reference room of the local library, where, shelved behind protective steel-mesh netting, encyclopedias were to be had for the asking.

Long mahogany-topped tables covered the floor space and I would seat myself at one of them, usually in the company of friends or classmates. With my schoolbooks spread comfortably around me, I would get down to my English or physics homework.

During winter we shared the places with tramps who came in out of the cold and, with a book in front of them as camouflage, slept until closing time. Above the huge clock that was visible from every part of the room, a notice demanded 'Silence.' All our consultative conversations were conducted in whispers until it became necessary to seek further information from a friend across the room. Suddenly the quiet would be shattered by a plaintive cry; 'What do you make the answer to $x^2-4x+4=3x^2+12x-9$, Norman?'. This was usually followed by the noise of moving chairs, dropped books and an outburst of general chatter. The Librarian, a middle-aged bespectacled character who was both the custodian and dispenser of reference books as well as the watchdog of decorum, would rise up from behind his desk under the clock, look around wildly to ascertain the source of the sudden breach in the quiet and shout for immediate silence. Our youthful high spirits, already unnaturally curbed by the enforced discipline, would erupt into a crescendo of book-thumping, inkwell-tapping and catcalls, until the enraged Librarian would run amok from table to table issuing threats of instant ejection. At each turn he would be met with vociferous cries of outraged innocence until, red in the face, he would angrily resume his seat and sit glaring at us through his pince-nez, in helpless frustration. An unspoken armistice being declared, silence would abruptly descend on the room, broken only by the scratching of pens on paper, the resumption of quiet whispering and the snoring of the tramps who always slept through our minor revolutions. During the course of the evening, this drama would be enacted three or four times. Each of us knew how far we dare go in flaunting the Librarian's authority and we never exceeded beyond that point.

As we grew more responsible the Librarian became a good friend, sparing no effort in providing the sources of information we sought in our studies.

I never achieved the distinction of becoming a 'college-boy'. At the age of fourteen I was awarded both an Art and Technical scholarship. Discreet asking around by my parents elicited the information that Art was a far from lucrative career for a Jewish boy, involving as it did years of unremunerative study with no prospect of a good safe job at the end of it. Finally I was enrolled as a student at a school in Fleet Street, where for two years I learnt the theory and technology of Process Engraving. This was followed by a five-year apprenticeship in the craft. Despite my parents' hopes and dreams for my future, a year after the completion of my indentures I found myself in the ranks of the great unemployed.

Borscht for the Breadwinner

August was a happy month for children. For five or six weeks from the end of July schools were closed for the summer holidays. During this period the lucky ones were able to spend a fortnight by the sea or in the open countryside. For those less fortunate, the local parks or the murky waters of the Regent's Canal served as a substitute. Seekers after knowledge found their outlet in the local museums or even further afield in the far West where the world's treasures were stored in glass cases and neatly described on labels. Sometimes a good-hearted teacher would lead these expeditions, giving up part of his or her hard earned leisure to do so. For me, summer was a time to visit my father's workshop, meet his work-mates, and enjoy the many treats the occasion provided.

★   ★   ★

One morning during school holidays my mother said to me, 'Be a good boy and take to daddy his dinner and be careful how you cross the road'. It was summertime and the sun shone out of a clear blue sky. The streets were full of children enjoying their freedom from lessons, playing cricket with lampposts or bollards serving as improvised wickets. Balls whizzed dangerously through the air and the occasional tinkle of shattered glass indicated the presence of a budding Jack Hobbs in their midst. But I had more important things to do. In a basket which I proudly carried over my arm, was a jam-jar full of borscht with chunky slices of beetroot floating in it. Wrapped up in a page of the *Jewish Zeit* (Morris Myer Ed.) were two slices of rye bread spread with chickenfat and sprinkled with salt together with a wedge of casseroled beef. This was to be my father's lunch which I had to deliver before one o'clock.

His workshop was about a mile and a half's walk away and I had three-quarter's of an hour to do it. I wandered down the side turnings seeking the cool shadows, my nostrils titillated by the odour of the chickenfat rising in the heat. In Boreham Street I stopped to watch a button-maker at work in her front room; she knew me well since my mother, a dress-maker, was one of her regular customers. She greeted me casually and continued with her work.

Further down the road I pushed my nose up against the saltbeef shop window and saw the sandwiches being prepared in readiness for the imminent lunch period. Giant pickled cucumbers floated like museum specimens in large glass tanks on the counter, and the hunger-provoking spiciness of the hot beef made my mouth water and sent me on my way. Turning the corner towards Club Row, the hiss of rollerskates on the ashphalt roadway informed me that I had only a few hundred yards to go before reaching my dad's factory. Of course the antics of the skaters held my attention for a time, so that it was with about five minutes to spare that I entered the warm, woodsmelling interior of the cabinet-making works.

I was greeted by an earsplitting scream of the cutting and planing machines ploughing their way through planks of mahogany. Chips of wood were flying through the air like an arctic blizzard and settled on the ground surrounding the machines in pinky mounds. The men that operated them wore flat peaked caps covered in a layer of sawdust that made me think of the sugar-coated sponge-cakes in Kossoff's bakery.

The foreman came over and greeted me. 'It's Morris's boy,' he shouted to all and sundry. 'Go up to your daddy.' I walked up a flight of ladder-like steps through which I could see the machines sucking in the long planks of wood like an Italian his beloved spaghetti. On the first floor finished wardrobes, dressing tables, dining tables and sideboards were awaiting transportation to the French polishers. This process was not carried out on the premises because of the sawdust which covered everything in sight.

A further flight of stairs led me direct to my father's bench. My arrival was observed by his fellow-worker and landsman, Yankel, who said; 'Morris, your boy is here, bless him'. My father was in the process of cutting dovetails in a wardrobe drawer. He wore a sawdust coated flat cap, a glue-flecked, once white apron, which despite a hundred boilings in our wash-copper at home, looked like a soft piece of white oak. Over an old flannel shirt he sported an unbuttoned grey waistcoat which held his folding rule, flat carpenter's pencil and a packet of Rizla cigarette papers.

The second floor was the workshop proper. Here under a grimy black-raftered roof, the cut and planed planks of mahogany, walnut or oak were lovingly and with great skill and craftsmanship fashioned into beautiful pieces of furniture. It was in places such as this, that many of the directors of todays' famous furniture companies learned the ABC of their craft. It was here that my father together with six other journeymen, spent his working day from 7.30 am to 7 pm cutting, glueing, joining, veneering his beloved pieces of wood, until the final dowel was driven home and the completed article taken to the polishers. Most of the tools he used were made by himself the steel plane blades and chisels tempered in a local blacksmith's furnace. My persistent memory of this workfloor is the smell of glue, men's sweat and the incense of resinous sawdust against the susurrus of crisp shavings spiralling out of a jackplane.

Despite my presence, my father conscientiously continued making his dovetails until the factory siren sounded the break for lunch. In the immediate and sudden silence that followed, he would carefully replace his mallet and chisel into a wall rack, pull out a couple of saw-scarred trestles from under his bench and place a plank across them so that we could sit down. It was at that moment that he would greet me with a kiss and take the basket of food which I still carried. Invariably Yankel would come over and join us.

My father was a short, wiry man without a superfluous ounce of fat on him. He ate sparsely so that I often shared his repast. This occasion was no exception. I had my fill of the cold borscht which my mother made so well, followed by a meat sandwich of carraway-seeded rye bread. Yankel contributed a lump of lokshen pudding so that even my eager appetite was sated. Meanwhile, a kettle had replaced the glue-pot on the gas-ring and a battered teapot stood ready to receive its libation of boiling water. I was sent downstairs to wash out three drinking glasses and, on my return, watched Yankel pour our tea whilst my dad cut a lemon into thin even slices with a small handsaw. We drank the hot astringent liquid through a cube of sugar held between the teeth.

When the eating and drinking was over. Yankel and my father would pull the peaks of their caps down over their eyes, stretch out on the bottom carcase of a wardrobe and go to sleep. I would replace the knife, fork and spoon together with the empty jam-jar into the basket in readiness for the trip back home. Now would follow my moment of supreme joy. From the shavings on the floor I would seek out some small off-cuts of wood. These I would cut, shape, glue and nail into two-winged aeroplanes or a three-funnelled warship complete with masts and guns. My father kept an old handsaw in his toolbox for my exclusive use on these

occasions. I was allowed to use his hammer, glue and sandblock. All chisels were strictly taboo as were the planes. The results of my labours were later to be displayed for the envy of my friends whose fathers were mere tailors, furriers or greengrocers.

All too soon the second siren called the faithful back to work. The sawmill below stairs began its infernal yowling and screaming: the workers on the second floor took up their planes and hammers, gluepots hissed and bubbled. Yankel returned to his bench and my father rolled a cigarette using his Rizla paper and a sprinkling of British Oak shag. Before lighting it he kissed me goodbye and told me to go over and show Yankel my handiwork. Yankel patted me on the head and said: 'Please God, you will be a good cabinet-maker like your father when you grow up.' He also kissed me and gave me a halfpenny to spend on ice-cream. I picked up the basket, now containing my home-made toys as well as the cutlery and the borscht-stained jam-jar, and walked down the stairs past the silent unpolished suites of furniture, past the screeching sawmill and out into the sunshine of the street. At the corner of Club Row, I bought a large vanilla wafer at Moss's, which by carefully controlled licking lasted all the way home.

The Club

Friendship was deep-rooted and flourished abundantly. Lack of privacy contributed to this cause, making one's personal sorrows or joys plain for all to see and share. Despite perennial poverty, no one was allowed to go hungry or unattended when sick. The strongest bond existed between immigrants who hailed from the same countries and towns abroad. They formed themselves into small groups or clubs where over glasses of lemon-tea problems were discussed and well-founded advice dispensed. Later they added cultural activities, inviting knowledgeable speakers to inform them on politics, music, literature and other subjects about which they knew little or nothing. They also played endless games of chess, draughts and dominoes which often continued from week to week and made regular attendance a necessity. Newcomers to the quarter were introduced with great ceremony and invited to establish themselves among the regulars. It was also here that new jobs were made known and old ones exchanged. The spoken word was Yiddish, the comradeship—universal.

*　　*　　*

Sunday evening my mother said to me, 'We are going to the Club tonight. So wash the face and comb the hair properly'. Most Sundays when we were not visiting relatives my parents went to the Club. The premises consisted of a large entrance lounge leading down a few steps to a hall. The situation was just off the City Road. Here it was always warm and friendly. A marble-topped counter greeted you as you came in through the swing doors. This supported a large samovar and plates of sandwiches and cakes. It was from this eldorado that we would later regale ourselves with buttered platzels, roll-mops and astringent lemon tea. Once inside the place my father would recognise one of his many landsmen who were members and take us over to share his table. I would be sent to the bar where Laszlo the Hungarian and his wife ran the refreshments. At my request he would hand me a box of dominoes which my father emptied onto the oilcloth tablecover in readiness for a game.

Later in the evening other friends would join the group and the air over the table would be thick with smoke and alive with conversation. A hand-written notice on the wall informed the reader that a concert would take place in the Hall at 9 o'clock. The son of one of the members was to play his violin accompanied by his sister at the piano. All were invited to listen.

The previous week we had heard a lecture on Shakespeare in Yiddish given by a little hunch-back man, who a year later, produced *A Midsummer Night's Dream* by the Bard, which we acted on the lawn of a stately home by moonlight.

By now the various games would be in full swing round the room. The silent and thoughtful chess enthusiasts, head in hand, gazing intently at the board; the cry of triumph from an over-excited draughts player whose trap had enabled him to sweep the board of his opponent's men, and the steady hum of conversation and proffered advice from the kibbitzers at the domino tables. My father's first encounter had grown into a dozen people, where at adjoining tables, the women knitted and talked as their menfolk slapped the dominoes into geometric patterns.

Permission was asked and granted for us, the children, to go to the concert. But first we were to have some food and tea. This was invariably the high spot of the evening. It was our job to order and collect the refreshments from the bar and serve the players without interrupting the game. We carefully eased our way through the now full-to-overflowing room, and asked Laszlo for the requisite glasses of lemon tea with sugar separate on the saucer. When this was delivered, we returned for buttered platzels with roll-mops and onions. Our special treat was a large piece of strudel baked by Laszlo's wife, which we saved for 'afters' at the concert.

We ate our roll-mops, platzels and drank the boiling hot lemon tea, then rushed off into the hall downstairs where we were fortunate to find a couple of seats near the piano.

There were about sixty people in the audience all waiting for the music to begin. They didn't wait in silence because the noise of their conversation was deafening, and the smoke lethal.

Soon the night's chairman appeared on the tiny stage and the noise died down. He announced the programme and introduced the young violinist and his sister. For the next forty-five minutes we were entranced. The music became a magic carpet taking us away from the problems and pressures of the present. We floated in our dreams, coming down to earth occasionally for a quick mouthful of the strudel we had thoughtfully saved for the moment. When the final round of appreciative applause rewarded the concluding item, the chairman informed us that next Sunday at the same time, there would be a lecture on Yiddish poetry and songs to which everyone was welcome.

Excited by the music, we would push our way through the maze of tables back to our parents where, tired but happy, we watched the dominoes slowly forming a straggling skeleton in the centre of the table. Later, carried pick-a-back on my father's broad shoulders, I would return home and be put to bed.

Itchy Park

Set into the soot-shaded sector, like emeralds in a tarnished brooch, were the little local parks carpeted with smooth well-tended lawns and ancient trees growing under protective arrest behind painted bars, rescued from final degradation by innumerable bye-laws and 'Keep dogs on a lead' notices that greeted the passing visitor at every entrance. These smaller oases were in addition to the more majestic spreads of Victoria Park, Hackney Downs or London Fields and were usually to be found adjacent to a church, like Shoreditch Park with its pleasant walks and old graveyard of crumbling headstones and gothic tombs.

It was in places like these that the perspiring natives disported themselves during the heat of summer, seeking the cool shadows under the gnarled oaks that spread their rheumaticky limbs in benediction over them. Here they would eat their newspaper-wrapped sandwiches in between draughts of home-made lemon water and the endless gossip between neighbours, until the park keeper's curfew and plaintive 'Everybody out' started an exodus towards the oven-hot homes of the quarter with the prospect of a sleepless bug-ridden night in a suffocating airless bedroom.

Throughout the year wardens were employed by the municipal council to cut the grass, pot the flowerbeds and wage ceaseless war against the rubbish that was left behind by untidy patrons. Armed with a spiked pole, the park keeper would impale odd scraps of orange peel, paper bags and Woodbine packets forming a giant shishkebab which he would unspike into the nearest litter bin. The park was also a meeting place for the chronic unemployed who passed the ennui between 'signings on' at the local labour exchanges, studying the racing edition of the *Star*, *Evening News* or *Standard* before investing much of their 'dole' in 3d. bets, which were passed on to the local bookmakers via the furtive touts that stood on the street corner.

One of these parks was strictly taboo and avoided by the local natives. This was Christ Church gardens on the open Commercial Street and across the road from Spitalfields fruit market. Whenever any of our copper saucepans needed galvanising, mother would send me to her uncle Yakov Mendl, a skilled tinsmith, who would carry out the necessary treatment in his shop that reeked of acrid fumes that left a metallic taste on the tongue. He lived in Crispin Street, a side turning opposite Christ Church. My normal route to his shop was via Brick Lane and then down Fournier Street past the Barbican Mission to the Jews and across the tramlines of the main road. The public garden adjacent to Christ Church was known to everybody as 'Itchy Park'. Its seats were usually occupied by tramps in various stages of drunkenness. Some were stretched out horizontally, taking up a whole seat and sleeping under the cover of an opened-up newspaper. Others were drinking out of beer bottles and shouting incoherently. Winter or summer the place was always full of them, bundled up in numerous garments and carrying paper parcels of food scraps that they usually managed to scrounge among the detritus of the fruit market across the road.

I never discovered why this particular park was a tramps' rendezvous. We children were always warned to keep well away from the place under threat of immediate retribution by one's parents or the possibility of being attacked by one of the drunks. The more daring among us would venture through the entrance and yell out 'Itchycoo' and then run for our lives as one or more of the tramps would stagger to his feet and lurch towards us swinging a bottle like a Crusader's mace, whilst a stream of invective accompanied the action. I invariably kept these little adventures to myself, merely mentioning Yakov Mendl's prognosis for our copper saucepan and the timing of the treatment. If my mother had ever suspected that I had gone into Itchy Park, she would have dipped me into a bath of boiling water and deloused my hair with all the specifics at her disposal.

Visiting
Cards

Leisure time was usually of short duration and manifested itself in one of three ways. You stayed home catching up on the accumulation of odd jobs impossible to tackle during the working week, because of sheer physical tiredness after a twelve hour daily stint at the bench. Alternatively, you put on your Sabbath suit or dress and descended on a nearby relative who resided in the native quarter. Here you had 'a bite to eat', followed by a heated discussion on world affairs or the rising cost of kosher meat in Mrs Zacharoff's butcher shop. Finally there was the weekly game of Solo, played at home or away, the same quartet matching their card skills closely observed by a vociferous group of kibbitzers. Whatever your choice of diversion, Sunday was the day you practised it.

★   ★   ★

'Comb your hair properly and wash the knees', said my mother to my sister and me. It was Sunday afternoon in the Mittel East and we were off to visit my mother's cousin and his family, who lived a penny tramride away. Uncle Simon, as we children called him, was a high class ladies' tailor, a short stoutish man, whose moon-shaped face, bisected by a huge buffalo-horn moustache, gave him a fierce appearance which belied his warm, generous nature. He rented a three-storied house in the basement of which was his workshop. On our arrival it was here we discovered him, sitting cross-legged on a high cutting table finishing off a 'special'. Being self-employed his working hours were dictated by the pressure of orders.

At the further end of the room a table had been laid for tea and as we entered voices of other guests could be heard chit-chatting to Simon and each other. We children were soundly hugged, kissed and cheek-pinched by the assembled adults and then left to play in peace with the surrounding appurtenances of Simon's craft.

With an audible sigh, Simon completed the last stitch of the costume he had been working on and draped it around one of the three pin-scarred dummies standing on their tripods in the corner. He covered it with a once-white dust sheet and joined the group now seated round the table. Tea was served by Auntie Golda, his wife. This involved the passing round of plates of schmaltz herring, smoked salmon on black bread, poppy-seed rolls coated with cream cheese, and finally the thick slices of cinnamon-veined yeastcake without which no self-respecting hostess in the Mittel East would dare set her table.

We all ate heartily and washed the food down with large cups of milky tea poured from a huge enamel teapot kept hot on the press-iron stove near the fireplace. As the men lit their cigarettes the table was cleared, the original white cloth replaced by a green plush model. Simon ceremoniously produced a pack of cards as the contestants arranged themselves for the weekly game of Solo.

I was too young at the time to understand the intricacies of the game. I can call to mind the mysterious cries of 'prop' and 'cop'; or the exotic and rare 'misere ouvert', the caller's face white with tension and excitement; or the bombastic 'abundance declared' collecting tricks in every round and snapping them down in line with martial precision; or the more frequent 'Solo' embarking on his private enterprise, with the non-playing kibbitzers urging him to draw trumps or lead from strength. Running through each shuffle and deal, like the refrain to a popular song, was the accusing cry of 'Who didn't put in the kitty yet?' Each player was interrogated in turn until the culprit was discovered. His penny was thrown on the table with an angry gesture, usually backed with the statement of 'By my life, I put in already!'

It was in the 'prop' and 'cop' calls that tempers would grow short. Someone had a blase queen schippa (whatever that meant), or a terrible hand with not one picture let alone a trump. Partner would be rude to partner, the insults growing stronger as the interval between them grew shorter until one of the players, goaded beyond endurance, would snatch up his stake money and say 'I've had it enough, already!' This was the signal for the breaking up of the game.

The subsequent inquest, however, would go on for hours, each player's weaknesses unmercifully revealed by his partner.

'You played that hand like a cripple.'

'Listen who's talking there, mine champion I don't tink! She's got six small trumps and doesn't lead mit a singleton nine of diamonds and I'm sitting there like a golem with the ace and jack in mine hand.'

'Now all of a sudden he's clever, mine Einstein; so why didn't you tuckeh draw trumps and let me make my jack and queen? Believe me, mine enemies should have such a partner. Next week, better you should go to the pictures instead.'

The most scathing remarks were reserved for the Solo calls which produced four overtricks. 'Solo, he calls. He's sitting there with the ace, queen, jack, ten of trumps, together with the ace, king of diamonds AND a blase ace of kreutz. A bloody liberty taker, he should make such a call. If you are so hard up for money, I will lend you some. You had it an abundance declare, there. That's what you should have called.' Since neither of my parents played cards, they were officially recognised as mediators between the warring factions. Soon, thanks to their tactful endeavours, an uneasy truce would be established, but the careless rapture of the early evening never returned.

We children, now somewhat tired and fretful, were overcoated and launched on an obligatory voyage of kissing the adults 'goodnight'. My parents in turn thanked Simon and Golda for their hospitality and gathered us up for the trek across the quarter. Both my sister and I would fall asleep in the tram, dreaming of tomorrow's sweets or ice cream made possible by the unexpected windfall of a penny pressed into our hands by Uncle Simon as we said 'goodnight'.

Playing the Game

Athletic pursuits, although never encouraged by the senior natives, were the leisure-time activity of their young. The narrow cobble-stoned streets of the quarter became the playing fields on which rival teams fought their homeric battles showing mercy to none. During summer, cricket was in the ascendant. From a wicket chalked on a lamp-post, the skilful batsman could hit the ball to his heart's content and still avoid breaking the fragile windowpanes that surrounded him on either side of the street. In winter, football was the game. A small rubber ball substituted for the unattainably expensive leather-pannelled sphere. Every tenement had its 'regulars' and Sunday afternoon fixtures were arranged attracting a good turn-out of both teams and supporters. The latter lined the pavements and encouraged the players with threats, four-letter words and energetic arm-waving.

Midway through the season the better players achieved a sought-after notoriety and were borrowed by rival outfits to strengthen their position in the field. In exchange for their services the 'stars' would be awarded a complete set of currently popular Pinnace cigarette cards, consisting of real photographs of professional footballers or alternatively, a pile of magazines which included *The Magnet*, *Gem*, *Sexton Blake* and the many-paged Nelson Lee booklets. Apart from the physical pleasure involved in the sport there was the added frisson of imminent danger engendered by the surprise appearance of a policeman on his beat. This would stop the game in mid-kick, everyone scrambling out of sight into the nearest doorway or alley. Some of the 'bobbies' were good sports who quickly made themselves scarce. Following his departure the teams would emerge from hiding and continue the game with renewed verve.

★   ★   ★

'A big deal' said my mother when I informed her that I had been chosen to play for the street football team. 'Mind the toe-caps of the shoes shouldn't be torn.' It was a Sunday afternoon in October with the light still good enough for a couple of hours' play. I was dressed in a long hand-knitted blue jersey with an orange roll-neck collar, the short trousers of my grey school-suit, grey knee-length stockings and my glacé kid everyday shoes. We were playing the Chambord Street Rovers on their own ground which was just round the corner from where I lived. When I arrived at the rendezvous, there were quite a few spectators hanging about waiting for the game to begin. The goalposts at either end of the pitch consisted of heaped up clothing (jackets, scarves, over-coats, etc.) guarded by the watchers, whose job it was to snatch them up and away at the first sign of the 'law's' approach.

I greeted our captain who was held in great respect by the assembly since he actually played for his school first eleven. The rest of us, by comparison, were mere enthusiasts who enjoyed the rough and tumble of the game, sporting our battered bare knees and bruised shins like medals of valour at the Cenotaph. A roll-call revealed that both teams were a man short. Two impartial spectators volunteered to stand in for them and now awaited selection. Both were unknown quantities as players. 'Go Pudden and Beef' said our captain. This was the time-honoured method of choosing an extra player in any team game, and was common practice beyond the confines of the quarter. The couple would agree among themselves who was to be Pudden and who Beef, and would respond accordingly. The selectors tossed a coin (Heads or Tails?), or flicked a cigarette-card (Back or Pic?), the winner having first choice.

We positioned our newly acquired reserve and the game was ready to start. Being a bit tall for my age, I played full-back where my size rather than skill acted as a mild deterrent to the opposition. The referee, a whistle-owning Scout, blew it for attention and ceremoniously placed a dirty tennis ball at the feet of the Chambord Street captain, who had won the toss for kick-off. At the second short blast of the whistle the game began.

The ball was dribbled, kicked, passed and punted from foot to foot to the accompaniment of jeers and cheers from the kerb-line spectators. It rapidly became apparent that we were the stronger team thanks to our captain's know-how. He soon proved his mastery of the art by executing a clean run through the opposition to score our first goal. This was greeted with wild applause by our supporters and cries of 'Offside' and 'Foul' from the 'enemy'. We bunched together, ready to defend our skipper's honour with fists if necessary. The referee and two nearby adults intervened on our behalf and the goal was made 'kosher'. The game resumed, but the careless rapture of the first kick-off was replaced by a 'needle' atmosphere which engendered a spate of kicked shins and over-vigorous savage tackling. Most of the forwards on both sides were soon limping badly and I nursed a bruised shoulder from a really nasty 'charge'. The glacé-kid toe-caps of my shoes showed the signs of the scuffing they had received both from abrasive contact with the kerbstone and the deliberate sabotage by foot-stomping indulged in by the enemy. Already possible excuses were forming in my mind to explain their condition to my mother and thus avoid her righteous wrath.

Meanwhile the game was hotting up with both sides putting on the pressure in their attempts to engineer a breakthrough. Again it was our captain who brilliantly scored his second goal. We were now two in the lead, and our frustrated opponents were desperately kicking everything in sight. One by one, our forwards hobbled to the kerbside to nurse bruised shins, aching ankles and grazed-to-bleeding kneecaps. We gave as good as we got so that both teams averaged about eight a side for the rest of the game.

It was just after halftime when one of the copper watchers cried 'Weenie'. This was the red alert signalling the approach of a policeman. In seconds, the coats were snatched up and the players hidden in hospitable doorways. The street, apart from a stray cat foraging in an open dustbin and the groups of spectators chatting nonchalantly, presented an innocent normality. From my hiding place I watched the policeman cross the road and walk in my direction. When he was almost on top of me I recognised him as the father of one of my school friends. He was boxing champion of 'H' Division, and essentially a friendly man. He stopped with his back to the door behind which I was hiding. 'Who's winning, lad?' he asked.

'We are', I replied nervously, mindful of previous painful encounters with the law. 'Good,' he said 'and mind none of you break any windows or I'll have the lot of you inside.' Still gazing away from me, he walked the length of Chambord Street and disappeared in the direction of the Virginia Planter, where no doubt the publican would regale him with a pint of bitter on the sly.

With his departure the 'goalposts' were quickly restored and the game resumed. We played on, confident of ultimate victory and indulged in all the flashy tricks of the trade in emulation of our current heroes who dazzled the crowds at Tottenham and Clapton Orient.

When the final whistle blew we were three goals ahead, an occasion of great satisfaction to us and of intense mortification to the defeated, who were even given the cold-shoulder by their erstwhile supporters. We limped our way home, still excited by the highlights of the game and its victorious outcome thanks to our captain on whom we showered praises for the part he had played in it. When I reached home, it was almost dark and the lamplighter was already on his nightly round, his lighting-pole aslant on his shoulder like a pike carried by the Beefeaters in the Tower of London.

Stardust

The first generation stemming from the early settlers were born and nurtured in the quarter, where they slowly assumed the characteristics of the native environment, at the same time, through education and contact, becoming more and more aware of life outside the narrow limits of their neighbourhood. Visits to the West End of the town, when funds permitted, revealed a facet of living which, whilst foreign to their strict upbringing, held for them a strange fascination. The bright lights, theatres, cinemas, restaurants lavish with red plush banquettes and parchment-shaded chandeliers, all were eloquent of the dolce vita, an unattainable dream to the dwellers in the Mittel East. Since it was a costly pilgrimage for Mahommed to visit the mountain, the mountain was brought to Mahommed. Wherever a hall or room of a suitable size was available, a social group would hire it for a Saturday night dance. Here, for a small entrance fee, the native son and daughter could meet, dance and fraternise with others of their kind. It was in such places that love and marriage flourished.

★   ★   ★

'Hurry up, Jack will be here in a minute', said my mother. It was Saturday night in the Mittel East and I was going to my first dance in the company of a friend. I was dressed up fit to kill and half a tin of vaseline had been rubbed into my unruly locks to help flatten them onto my skull.

Jack arrived in time. He was three years my senior and an old-timer in the dance halls having won several competitions. He was to be my guide and mentor for the evening. I had been reluctant to go but pressure from my mother, aided and abetted by Jack, had overruled my lack of enthusiasm.

We walked to the hall which was situated on a main road in the heart of the quarter. We paid our entrance fee at the door where the organisers sat behind a rickety card table doling out the tickets. For 1s. 6d. we could dance and partake of light refreshments during the interval. The hall had a lived-in look. It was much used for the celebrations of weddings and wealthy barmitzvahs. The walls were distempered pink with alternate panels of floral wallpaper and mirrors along them. At the further end on a raised platform, the band, piano, violin, saxophone and drums were already beating out a foxtrot. Gold-painted wooden-framed chairs lined the complete perimeter of the hall and were occupied by girls and boys not yet involved in the dance. The general lighting was subdued and emanated from numerous parchment-shaded candelabra that jutted out at six foot intervals round the walls. The piece de resistance was suspended from the centre of the ornately plastered ceiling by a chain. This was a globe eighteen inches in diameter covered completely with tiny squares of mirrored glass. At regular intervals the band would play a slow waltz. Immediately, the house lights would be doused and a beam of light, projected from a lantern on the stage, would play on the globe which rotated to throw fragmented reflections of the spectrum on the gliding couples below. After the waltz and throughout the evening the globe would continue to spin on its own momentum, twinkling in the houselights like a constellation gone mad.

Jack pulled me by the arm and said 'Come over and be introduced'. Self-consciously, I crossed the parquet floor at his side, my shoes squeaking above the chatter like provoked mice. I met three fellows I knew from the neighbourhood and five girls who were strangers. One of them was sorted out for me. She was about 5ft 6in tall, had jet black hair cut fashionably in an Eton crop, a beautiful olive skin and wore a vermilion coloured dress that reached to her knees. During our introduction she kept swaying around in her seat to the rhythm of the band until Jack whispered, 'Ask her to dance'. I did so with all the aplomb I could muster, took her into my trembling arms, stepped out resolutely and promptly trod on her foot. Until that moment all my dance partners had been male friends who were proficient enough in the art to tutor me. Suddenly to encounter a soft pliable warm back instead of the customary tweed or worsted of my teachers, made me forget all I had gleaned from them. Betty smiled up at me bravely and suggested that we sit this one out. We resumed our places where I confessed, face aflame, that she was the first girl I had ever tried to dance with. She immediately smiled and said, 'Let's have another try'. It was a waltz. The lights were switched off and the lantern beam projected on the mirrored sphere. Betty stood up and limped into my arms. George Raft was ready for her. With a smooth gliding step I swung into the one-two-three of a slow dreamy waltz, 'I wonder why you keep me waiting Charmaine, my Charmaine?' Betty sang. Stars were showering down on us from the ceiling. Through the susurrus of shuffling shoes on the polished floor I could hear the violin taking up the theme. We floated on in our own fantasies until the number ended and the light returned. 'You dance nicely', said Betty. I walked back to our seats a foot off the ground.

A sudden roll on the drums and the tea interval was announced. A door opened at the side of the stage wall, revealing a trestle table placed across the opening behind which two girls were busily engaged in handing out cups of tea and plates of sliced cake. I joined the queue, giving Betty the opportunity to powder her nose in the Ladies. When I reached the counter I collected two large cups of tea and assorted cakes and made my way back to Betty, who looked lovelier than ever after her freshen up. We drank our tea and finished the cake. The empties were put under our chairs, where they remained for the rest of the evening.

When the band came back, the dancing resumed. We waltzed, foxtrotted, one-stepped, two-stepped and sat out a Russian Cossack novelty dance performed by the more energetic in our midst. As the last waltz was tinkling on the piano and the stars showered down on our heads, I bravely snatched a kiss from Betty's upturned face and danced in the clouds.

Later I said good-bye to everybody, thanked Jack for getting me to go to the dance, and waited for Betty to come out of the cloakroom. She appeared with her dancing shoes carried in a brown paper bag. I went to many dances after that occasion, alone or with others from the quarter, but I never met Betty again.

Love Thy Neighbour

In the native quarter a good neighbour was worth his or her weight in gold. Day to day living under severe economic pressures made the borrowing of foodstuffs or even small amounts of money to tide things over until the breadwinner received his weekly stipend, a necessity. In time of sickness one's neighbour would, without a moment's hesitation, take over the household duties of the unfortunate invalid, cook meals for the family and see the children off to school. All this in addition to her own onerous responsibilities. No extravagant thanks were given or expected for the good deed. It was just a part of life in the quarter and it worked on a reciprocal basis. Tomorrow, God forbid, your neighbour could fall sick and you would step into the breach, cooking for her husband, washing and feeding her children, seeing them safely to and from school, and putting them to bed after supper.

News travelled from neighbour to neighbour, and was exchanged at the butchers or over the backyard fence. Forthcoming pregnancies, marriages, engagements and day to day gossip were grist to the mill. Secrets were passed on in Russian or Polish and spread in Yiddish. Living in tightly-packed communities, privacy was a luxury enjoyed by a fortunate few and this privilege was too often regarded with suspicion

by the deprived mass. Despite its nearness to the Metropolis with its sophisticated way of life, the quarter was a substitute village for most of its inhabitants, and they lived their lives accordingly.

★   ★   ★

'Go next door by Mrs Polinsky and borrow for me a cup milk', my mother said to me. It was midsummer at the time, and mother had let our can go sour and Jones' dairy across the road was already shut up for the afternoon. I took a cup off the dresser, walked down two flights of stairs to the street and then through the passageway next door into Mrs Polinsky's kitchen. Like our house, the place was unbearably hot. All the doors and windows were open, but not a breath of air stirred. Mrs Polinsky was seated by the window darning the family's socks. She looked up and greeted me, 'How's the mummeh?' she asked. I said she was alright thankyou, and could we please have a cup of milk until to-morrow morning. Mrs P. got up with a groan and fetched the metal milk-can which was kept under the kitchen sink immersed in a pail of cold water, and carefully filled a cup. 'Here you are and take it in good health. Tell the mummeh I will send back the Hudsons powder tomorrow, please God, after breakfast.' I took the milk, thanked her, and returned home to deliver the message.

My mother was preparing supper which consisted of bowls of sour milk with sliced cucumber and spring onion cut into them. A saucepan containing tiny new potatoes was boiling away on the gas stove. These would be served in a large dish coated with butter, to be eaten with the sour milk. My father was already home from work, summer being the slack season in the cabinet-making trade. He was washing at the kitchen sink and obviously enjoying the cooling effect of the cold water.

'I heard today that the shickseh, the ginger across the road, is again pregnant,' said my mother as she sliced up a large loaf of brown bread with the Bakers' Union seal still stuck on the crust. 'It's the second time in two years. Believe me, it's a shame for her mother.'

Having imparted this piece of vital information, we sat down to eat after I called my sister in from the back yard where she had been playing with her doll. 'How's Mrs Pollock. She's better yet?'

Mrs Pollock lived next door to the Polinsky's. She was suffering from some obscure ailment and was confined to bed. Her husband was a cabinet-maker like my father and her two children were friends of my sister and myself. For the past two weeks my mother had been cooking meals for them, and at the same time nursing Mrs Pollock. This meant an endless day for my mother, having two families to cater and clean for, but it was the neighbourly thing to do. During the winter 'flu epidemic it was Mrs Pollock who had looked after us when mother was sick.

Almost every family in the quarter had a good neighbour willing to undertake the duties of nursing or cooking in any emergency. Here, 'Love thy neighbour' was not a religious text but a way of life. The disadvantages of living in close proximity and without privacy were outweighed by the warmth and friendship freely given by neighbour to neighbour.

Evening In

To most of us pleasure was merely a state of 'non-pain'. The deep-down satisfying emotion usually associated with the word was practically non-existent in the quarter. The daily struggle for a livelihood made certain of that. But for the young it became a possibility. An invitation to an 'evening-in' at the home of a girl-friend made the birds sing and the sun shine. The date was usually pencilled on the family calendar and the days counted down with impatience. Saturday evenings were the most popular, which left the Sunday for recovering from what was probably a late night's return home. Very often the girl hostess lived outside the quarter, which added a long walk to the occasion. When the day was nigh, all hell broke loose in the invitee's household.

★   ★   ★

'Make sure you got a clean handkerchy', said my mother to me as I stood before the wardrobe mirror for about the tenth time, making certain that my trousers were at the correct height from my shoes. Since after tea I had been preparing myself for the 'evening-in' at a girl friend's house. She said to be there at eight, and a quick glance at the marble clock on the mantel showed it was almost time to leave. Bedecked in my blue-serge suit (Yomtov best) specially pressed for the occasion by mother, my feet sporting a pair of fashionable purple socks with white embroidered clocks up the sides, encased in black patent-leather shoes. A hand-knitted silk tie so tightly knotted into the shirt collar that my breathing was partially impaired completed my ensemble. My normally curly locks were smarmed down on my scalp like a second skin. Another quick, reassuring glance in the mirror, a hasty kiss from my mother who said, 'Enjoy yourself and be a good boy', and I was out of the house en route for Stamford Hill where my current beloved lived in spacious splendour.

For the uninitiated, an 'evening-in' was a party. Usually the invitee was a girl and the company would consist of couples 'going steady' or of possibles who with a bit of a push could be paired off on a more permanent basis. Should any guest fail to turn up, then a last-minute panic call was put out to balance the sexes.

A long tram ride from the quarter brought me to my destination, and after giving my shoes a quick polish on the sides of my trousers, I rang the door-bell.

The door was quickly opened by my girl-friend who must have observed my approach through the elegant lace curtains across the window. She greeted me self-consciously and invited me in. I was led into the front room which was as large as our entire flat in the quarter, and introduced to several early arrivals who were conversing round the gramophone cabinet. I recognised some of them and mumbled a conventional 'Pleased to meet you' to the strangers. We stood about and chatted, listening to Layton and Johnson's latest recording.

By 8.30 pm all the guests had arrived and were dancing with joyful abandon to the tempo of the Denza Dance Band. I struggled manfully through a quickstep, inflicting permanent injuries on all who crossed my path. An hour later, exhausted but hungry, we were ushered into an adjoining room where a huge dining table, lavishly spread with titillating foodstuffs, awaited our pleasure. Again the couples paired off to indulge in banter, bagels, platzels, pretzels and assorted sandwiches. Bottles of lemonade, sealed with a glass ball, were pressed into surrendering their fizzy contents. There were brownstone bottles of ginger beer and the ever popular kola.

By now, even the most inhibited among us had warmed up to the party adding his or her noise to the conversation and laughter that fought successfully against the music issuing from a swan-neck loud speaker resting atop of the two-valve radio in the corner. Eventually replete, we were urged to return to the front room for fun and games. This was the piece de resistance of the evening's programme. The games played ranged from Charades to Postman's Knock, and many a tenderfoot enjoyed his first kiss and cuddle in the merciful dark of the passage outside the front room. The girls blushed and giggled; the men acted nonchalantly, attempting to emulate the suave detachment of Rudolph Valentino or John Barrymore.

At regular intervals, someone would sit down at the piano and play.

One by one the couples would get up from their armchairs or cushioned sofas and join the dance, dreaming and swaying to the haunting strains of 'Charmaine' or 'In a Little Spanish Town twas on a Night Like This!' The girls, enveloped in their own fantasies, eyes closed, would sing as their partners led them through the sweep and turn of the tinkling waltz.

Later, cups of hot tea were handed round, together with plates of cheese cake, strudel and apple-pie. The chatter went on incessantly and dates were made. Around midnight the gaslight, which had been turned down to a mere glimmer after the tea interval, was restored to its normal brilliance and was followed by the surreptitious wiping away of lipstick transferred with great pleasure during the hour of darkness. This was a signal for the party to break up. Many of us, including myself, faced the prospect of a long trek home, the last tram having departed a good while ago. But it was worth it. We said our goodbyes and thank you for a wonderful evening, snatched a last kiss in the deserted street outside, after which I boldly stepped out into the darkness, like the hero in the fade-out of a romantic film.

The Turn

'Lebensraum' was a commodity in short supply. Each sooty-bricked dwelling housed three or four families distributed in the ratio of one family to a floor. The interiors were gloomy or downright dark and each level, separated by a flight of steep uncarpeted wooden stairs, terminated at a bannistered landing or 'passidge' into which the doors of the flat opened. A small lavatory patronised by all the tenants above street-level was usually sited on the first floor. Anyone not suffering from a nasal cold could find it in the dark without difficulty.

In order to save one's parents the chore of trampling up and down the stairs each time a child demanded entry by thumping the black cast-iron knocker on the street door (a knock for each floor was the signal), it was kept wide-open. The prevailing wind would blow dust, pieces of newspaper, straw and empty Woodbine packets into the passageway. Through the same street door, stray cats would drag in fishheads from the neighbourhood shop and leave them to phosphoresce in the dark. They also used the place as a convenience. To combat this onslaught of dirt, detritus and cats, the tenants established a rota for scrubbing down the stairs, passages and lavatory on a fixed day of the week. This operation was known as 'The Turn', and the obligation to fulfil it, sacrosanct.

★　　★　　★

One morning during school holidays, my mother said to me, 'Be a good boy and do the Turn for me today'. In our tenement the Turn meant scrubbing down two flights of stairs, the lavatory on the first floor, three passageways and hearthstoning the front doorstep. Apart from the prestige this would give me in the eyes of our fellow-tenants, I invariably received a penny reward for my labours.

First of all I swept all the way down two flights of stairs, the intervening passageways and the lavatory, which was always littered with torn newspaper or comics. The collected debris was emptied into the backyard dustbin. Meanwhile, my mother had prepared a pail-full of hot water into which she had put a liberal portion of Hudson's Powder and carbolic. Taking up a floorcloth, scrubbing brush and a bar of Lifebuoy soap, I commenced my labour of love. Starting outside our own front door I attacked each step vigorously, leaving a strong 'hospital' smell in the air as the drying out began.

When I had completed the first flight and reached the landing lavatory, our neighbour, Mrs Hollander, opened her kitchen door ostensibly to throw a little extra light on the job since at that level the place was in comparative darkness. Seeing me instead of my mother doing the Turn, she at once shouted into the room at her own children, 'Look what a good boy he is, bless him, doing the Turn for mudder. I should live to have such children. Not a finger do mine lift to help me.' If it was Friday (baking day), she would give me a large piece of yeast cake, still oven-warm. This was by way of being an extra to my penny payment.

Spirits boosted by the cake and compliments, I would tackle the odiferous toilet after carefully scrutinising its walls for recently inscribed graffiti. It was from these uninhibited records that one learned who was in love with whom. Entwined arrow-pierced hearts revealed that Hymie from downstairs was going steady with Sadie from next door and that Sarah Hollander had kissed Joe. A corroborative series of x's indicated the exact number of her embraces. The writing was generally done with indelible pencil that defied erasure. Prior to the landlord's annual visit of inspection, my father used to scrape down the door and sandpaper the walls clean.

Leaving the toilet a cleaner place than I had found it, my itinerary took me to the penultimate flight of stairs leading to the front door. Following in my wake, mother had spread sheets of newspaper over all the wet flat areas to prevent them being stepped upon before drying out. By this stage my enthusiasm would begin to wane, but inevitably revived at the thought of the hearthstoning to come. I scrubbed and swabbed the last yard of the hallway and then opened wide the heavy oak street door, which I had thoughtfully closed during the preliminary sweeping-up operation. Failure to do this would have resulted in the dirt being blown in faster than I could dispose of it.

Now visible to all and sundry, I attracted the attention of passing friends who besieged me with offerings of marbles, cigarette-cards, or gob-stoppers, to allow one of them to do the hearthstoning. With great deliberation I would consider the respective merits of each bribe, and finally hand over the brush and cloth to the successful applicant. Under my direction, he would wash the step and pavement, then apply and smooth on the whiting.

When the job was completed to everyone's satisfaction, the non-starters having remained to keep a critical eye on the winner, I would collect my dues and go back up the now practically dry stairs. In the gloom everything smelled of carbolic and newsprint. When I told mother that the Turn had been successfully carried out, she kissed me and took the promised penny out of her purse, which she handed over with a stern admonition 'not to spend it on rubbish'.

Polinsky's Horse

Animal life was essentially utilitarian. Dogs and cats were housed and fed so that they could deal with the rats and mice that infested the neighbourhood. The chickens that scratched the unyielding concrete of numerous back yards, were there to provide eggs or were swiftly transformed into lockshen soup for a Sabbath meal. Pets, as such, were regarded as a form of goishe madness, costing hard-earned money to keep and providing no tangible return for the outlay. After a time the natives did lower the barriers to caged birds, which they kept in small cages suspended from a nail in the brickwork immediately outside the backroom windows. Canaries were the favourites, and many a canny native augmented his meagre income by breeding them for subsequent sale. But it was the horse owner who carried the day by the sheer size of his charge. Between the shafts of a cart these animals were used to carry heavy goods of every kind, thus paying for their food and stabling, as well as providing a livelihood for their owners. A ride on a cart was a treat for the youngsters; to be permitted to hold the reins, a joy beyond compare.

★   ★   ★

Mr Polinsky was our next door neighbour. Because of the size of his family, he rented the complete house including the shop on the ground floor, the wide window of which was painted halfway up so that privacy was possible without excluding the light. Mr P. looked like Maxim Gorki, and invariably wore a leather jerkin which informed the knowledgeable passer-by that he owned a horse. Which he did. Bronco was the horse's name. I never knew how many hands high he was nor had the slightest idea of his species. He was chestnut brown all over and seemed to tower over me when I could be induced to feed him a few knobs of sugar out of my hand.

Every day Mr Polinsky drove his horse and van to market, where aided by his several sons, they sold boxes of assorted biscuits by the hundredweight to eager customers. The shop was used merely for storage of the stock. During school holidays, my sister and I would gladly assist the loading or unloading of the van, in exchange for which we received handfuls of custard creams or a ride behind Bronco to his stables around the corner. These were at the short end of Gossett Street. Once through the large timbered doors, one could imagine oneself back in the days of the stage coaches of Old England. There was a hayloft complete with pitchforks and bales of sweet-smelling hay. Chickens pecked away on the manure heap close by a giant shed housing the two large horsedrawn brakes which were hired for Sunday school outings to Chingford or Epping Forest. The brake was a form of rustic bus with built-in seating for about two dozen children or adults. With a pair of powerful horses between the shafts, resplendent in shining brasses, polished leather harness and straw-plaited manes, the brake was a thing of beauty and a joy to ride in. It was here that Bronco was stabled for the night in the company of two jet black horses which were used to draw wedding or funeral carriages.

One memorable morning, Mr Polinsky said to me 'Go ask the mother if you can ride with me to Epping market. It will for the whole day be, so bring with to eat'. It was during the school summer holidays, and the prospect of a long ride behind Bronco, apart from rousing the envy of my friends, would make an exciting change from street cricket or playing in the park. Having obtained my mother's permission and blessing, during which she prepared enough sandwiches to keep me going for a fortnight, plus a wine bottle filled with milk to wash them down, all of which was packed in a straw basket and handed over with the stern injunction to be a good boy and not to fall off the cart. This was followed by a quick wipe over with a damp face cloth and a swift kiss on the brow. I ran down the stairs as fast as the basket on my arm would permit. By the time I reached the street, Mr Polinsky's van was loaded, the large tins of biscuits neatly stacked to allow room for a pile of sacks on which I and his youngest son were to sit. Mr P., whip and reins in hand, was talking to Bronco in Yiddish, the horse stamping his hind leg impatient to get going. With a sharp cry of 'gee-up' we were off. From the back of the van I waved good-bye to my mother, who was watching our departure from the second floor bedroom window. The metal-hooped wheels grated on the cobblestone roadway and the floor of the van vibrated with every revolution. I could hear the rhythmic clipclop of Bronco's steel shoes as we wound our way through the streets of the quarter. When we rode over ashphalt or tar wood blocks the ride was smoother, but most of the way was cobblestoned. Our conversation en route was enhanced with a natural tremolo produced by the constant vibration. From over the tailboard I watched the streets and houses unwinding behind us. Soon we were in strange territory. The tenements had given place to large houses enclosed by high walls and beautiful front gardens visible through ornamental iron gates. Then suddenly nothing but green fields, hedges and trees as far as the eye could see.

'We're nearly there', said Moishe, who sat beside me on the sacks. We drove into the market, passing cattle pens filled with bleating sheep, mudstained pigs and young calves munching straw. We could smell the pigs a mile off. Finally, we reached the covered section where the Polinskys rented a stall. The journey had taken about an hour and a half. The place looked like Brick Lane with a roof over it. Stalls selling everything from clothes to hair pins were already set up and doing business. Mr Polinsky dismounted and unbolted the tailboard. From the back axle he unhooked a feed bag filled with oats which he strapped onto Bronco's head. We began unloading tins of biscuits which were arranged in tiers around the stall like galleries in a theatre. The lids were removed to reveal the contents, neatly packed in geometric splendour. From a wooden box Moishe produced a pair of scoop scales, assorted weights and paper bags, which were set up ready for action. I was handed a cushion-covered orange crate to sit on, and we were open for business. Box after box of biscuits were auctioned off and handed over to waiting customers. Trade was encouraged by a running commentary delivered by Mr. P.'s eldest son. A good crowd gathered round us, laughing at the sales talk and buying pounds and pounds of custard creams, Marie Osbornes, Chocolate Bourbons, Ginger Nuts, Shortbreads, etc., etc.

At midday, Mr Polinsky said, 'Eat now', I unpacked my sandwiches and set to. The long ride, fresh air and excitement had certainly not impaired my appetite. It was the milk that presented a problem. The heat of the day, together with the vibration of the cart, had plugged the bottleneck with creamy butter. I was sent to the nearby coffee stall to purchase a jug of tea. On my return, this was poured into tin mugs and drunk by the Polinskys in between sales.

For hours I sat by the stall watching the crowds moving around the market and making their purchases. Above the general hum of the conversation, I could hear the pigs squealing and the calves mooing, a fact which made me realise that I was a long way from the native quarter.

At dusk the market closed. Mr Polinsky went off to get Bronco whilst I assisted his sons, putting the lids back on the biscuits, collecting bags and replacing the scales and weights in their special container. When the cart arrived, we reloaded as before and settled in for the ride back home. Before setting off, one of the boys lit the oil lamps at the front and rear of the cart. The tailboard safely bolted to his satisfaction, Mr Polinsky mounted the driver's seat and ordered Bronco to 'Gee-up'. The cattle pens were empty as we passed them on our way out. In the gathering twilight the trees and hedges were silhouetted against the night sky, and birds would suddenly dart out of them as if shot from a catapult.

Soon the persistent clip-clop of Bronco's hooves and the gentle sway of the cart put Moishe and me to sleep. When we reached the native quarter, I was gently awakened by Mr Polinsky and lifted down to the pavement. He handed me my food basket, now filled with bags of assorted biscuits, and put a sixpence in my hand. 'Your wages', he said, and watched me walk my sleepy way home.

A Day Passes

The summer sun rose over the forest of chimneys that stretched across the rooftops of the native quarter, like pegs on a giant solitaire board. In the morning quiet, the muezzin cry of a celibate cockerel challenged the new day from his perch in some stony backyard. From my bedroom window on the second floor I watched the night sky fade in the morning sunshine. The alarm erupted in my parents' room, and I heard my father mutter under his breath as he plunged the mechanism into blissful silence. In front of me, the still undisturbed cabinet-making workshops slept behind their dirty window panes. The faint morning breeze brought a whiff of pine resin and glue to my nostrils. But these were mere ghosts of woods long past. Soon the bandsaws would be tearing through planks of mahogany and oak, bringing new smells to be enjoyed.

In the house next door, I could see our neighbour's wife already in the kitchen putting the kettle on for the family's tea. They would soon be down to breakfast. But first her youngest son Moishe and I would walk down Gossett Street to the Brick Lane end where Mrs Schwartz's bakehouse would sell us hot fresh rolls covered in poppyseed or crisp shiny bagels that my father enjoyed so much.

En route, we would pass Jones the milkman riding his float that resembled a Roman chariot, its giant churn and metal cans rattling on the cobble-stones like hail on a galvanised iron roof. Mr Jones would flick his whip in greeting, and if in a good mood, let us ride part of the way with him, or feed his horse a breakfast carrot or two.

Across the road, the fishmonger had taken down his shutters and lowered the sunblind over his open stall. In a moment he would hose down the large marble slabs on which the fresh fish would be displayed for his regular customers. The weather being hot, he would keep the fish boxed in ice chunks. He also set out rows of kippers impaled on iron bars which hung horizontally from chains fixed to the ceiling. But all the washing in the world would never dispel the overpowering smell that permeated the place like an invisible fog.

Next door, on the corner of Gibraltar Walk and Virginia Road, Jones's dairy was open for business. The cows in the stable at the back of the shop were being milked by Harry, each rhythmic tug of the teats producing a jet of milk into the galvanised bucket gripped between his knees.

Immediately opposite the dairy, and next door to the Virginia Planter, was Walker's catsmeat shop. The neighbourhood stray cats were waiting outside the door for possible titbits, but would be rewarded by a surprise dousing from a pail of water kept under the counter by Bert Walker for this purpose. I waited hopefully for action, but the Walkers were not yet up.

By now, the sun had driven the shadow from our side of the street and the bedroom windows were beginning to sport the inhabitants' blankets and uberdecks for their daily airing. Voices hurled out of the openings like stones frightened the sparrows scavenging on the manna provided by the milkman's horse.

Moishe had just called for me, and we were off to Mrs Schwartz's where the distilled essence of yeast and oven-fresh bread whetted the appetite and lowered sales resistance. I clutched my bag of still warm platzels and bagels, fighting back the temptation to nibble at one of them. An empty Nestle's milk tin lying in the gutter distracted me from my ethical problem. I kicked it along the road making some pretty sharp passes to Moishe, who returned the can to me. We were both proud of our apparent skill as potential candidates for the Spurs team. The noise caused one or two people to hurl a couple of curses our way, which added incentive to our efforts. Reaching home with the toe-caps of my boots scuffed by the tin and my appetite whetted by the matutinal exercises, I

sat down to breakfast prepared during my absence by my mother. A plateful of sour milk and cream cheese tasted delicious with the freshly buttered platzel. I enjoyed it.

Today was the last day of my school holidays. Tomorrow I would return to the routine of classes and homework. Today I was still free to roam the streets and make plans to visit the Bethnal Green Museum in

Cambridge Road. I'd go there when I had changed my library books in the building nearby.

After breakfast, my mother went downstairs to the communal wash kitchen to do the family laundry. It was a small cheerless place into which the sun never shone. The only window faced the backyard fence, which in turn was surrounded by workshops that cast a permanent shadow over it. In one corner there was a red-glazed sink with one large cold water tap above it. Diagonally opposite was the copper, set into a stone framework with a fireplace immediately under it. A fire was already burning in the grate, and the water in the cauldron bubbling in a cloud of steam. Various items of underclothing waiting to be washed, lay in a heap on the stone floor. A zinc bath, firmly planted on a heavy timber stool together with a washboard, awaited my mother's attention. She would ladle the boiling water into the bath with an old copper saucepan, empty a packet of Hudson's powder into it, and soak, soap and scrub each article of clothing before consigning them to the boiler. There was also a bleached copperstick that was used to immerse the laundry so that the heavily battened lid could be placed over the cauldron's mouth, and the boiling go on undisturbed. Later, the rinsing in cold water would follow. A tub of Reckitts Blue and Robin starch were brought into use as required. Then the great mangling operation began as the wooden rollers of our mangle were hand cranked, and the surplus water squeezed out of each individual piece of laundry to flood the stone floor until it gushed out of the special runnels like a river during a storm.

By midday, vests, shirts, sheets and socks would hang pegged from a line in the backyard. Smut and sawdust would settle on the damp surfaces before the drying was complete, and the struggle would begin again. I helped to carry water from the boiler to the bath, turned the mangle and fed the fire under the copper with blocks of wood brought back by the sackful from his workshop by my father. Later I helped mother to peg the heavy damp washing on the line. After midday dinner, I could go my own way with a trouble-free conscience, feeling that my freedom had been paid for in advance.

*   *   *

It was evening in the Mittel East. Already the cats were yowling on the backyard fences, and the sunset silhouetted the chimneys against the night sky, making them look like sticks of licorice. One or two barrow-men were still trundling their wares in the street below, and the clippety-clop of hooves on the roadway told me that our neighbour was back from market and ready to stable his horse for the night. The gas lights were hissing away in the kitchen across the way, and the lamplighter went his rounds in the street. At the corner of Virginia and Columbia Road, the pubs were open, and an early drunk was singing his wordless song. The sky darkened from azure to indigo, and the stars twinkled in the dark. A mile or so away, my father was still at work. He was lucky. Usually summer was a long slack period. But my father was working. I was already in bed listening to the night noises that filtered through the open window. I wondered if I would manage to stay awake until he came home —but I knew that when he did get back, I would be fast asleep.

Please God By Your Children

Birth, death and marriage were moments of great occasion. Each in turn was greeted with its appropriate pomp and ceremony, joy or tears, or tears of joy. It was marriage that cost the most and inevitably left a deep scar in the life-savings of the father who finally footed the bill. Yet blessed indeed were the parents whose daughter was about to embrace matrimony. At the right time, a script-set, gold-dusted, deckle-edged invitation card would be posted to family and friends stating the date, time and place of the ceremony, and of the banquet to follow. The front of the card was ornamented by the initials of the bride and groom, entwined like playful boa-constrictors into a strangulated lover's knot. Throughout the native quarter dressmakers would be busy making up silks and satins into beautiful dresses for the female recipients of invitations. Men's frock coats would be shaken free of mothballs, brushed and sponged, and hand-pressed by the local tailor. Top hats that had lain dormant on top of the family wardrobe since the last simcha, would be hustled out of hibernation, and the nap smoothed lovingly into an incredible sheen. On the day stated, the bride would be wed and guests fed.

$$\star \quad \star \quad \star$$

Sunday morning mother said to me 'It's time already to dress for the wedding. The carriage will soon be here'. Today was my aunt's wedding day, and my sister and I were to be bridesmaid and pageboy respectively. Our duty was to hold up the end of the long white train of her wedding dress as she entered the synagogue, and when she walked out of it on the arm of our uncle Jack to be.

For this special occasion, mother had made for me a most resplendent blue satin suit and knee breeches. I looked like Lord Fauntleroy when decked out in the complete outfit that included a Van Dyk hand-crochetted collar and cuffs, and glacé kid shoes with shining silver buckles. My long curly hair was drenched in brilliantine and combed into a centre parting that gave me a 'child Samuel' look as depicted on the milkman's calendar that hung on our kitchen wall.

My sister's dress was made to match my suit, as were her shoes to match mine. Her hair was naturally black and straight and had been done up into paper 'crackers', which when unfastened and combed out, produced a curly wave which was regarded as an aid to beauty. Having prepared us for the approaching ordeal, my parents dressed themselves in the ceremonial garments of the time.

Father, wearing the top hat and frock coat purchased for his own wedding many years previous, looked a majestic figure of a man in contrast to the old suit and flat sawdust-covered cap he wore to work each day.

Mother emerged from the bedroom transformed like Cinderella in the fairy tale. She wore a beautiful dress that was covered in flounces, pleats, fringes and lace. Her hair was combed into the then fashionable cottage-loaf style much favoured by Queen Mary. She wore her gold heart-shaped locket containing miniature photographs of her parents in Lida, and a heavy gold bracelet. She had daringly used Swansdown powder on her face, which gave off a delicate perfume.

Three knocks on the street door below indicated that the carriage had arrived. We descended the dark cat-smelling stairs and passageways until we reached the street below, where a crowd of neighbours stood waiting to wish us mazeltov. The carriage was a four-wheeler from Burns, with the driver sitting up front dressed in a gleaming top hat, a black frogged overcoat, top boots with natural suede uppers, and held a long flexible whip onto which a white silk bow was tied. The horse between the shafts was as black as night and beautifully groomed. These same carriages were also used for Christian funerals. Today we would move at a brisk trot instead of the slow-clip-clop of the sad occasion. With an authoritative 'Gee-up' from the driver, we rumbled off over the cobblestones towards my aunt's home in the very heart of the Mittel East, leaving a scented trail of brilliantine, mothballs and Swansdown powder in our wake.

On arriving at our destination, my mother, sister and I alighted from the carriage; my father was going on to the bridegroom's home in Flower and Dean Street. Upstairs in Auntie's place, the dingy flat had been turned into a colourful flower garden. A long dining table in the middle of the parlour groaned under the weight of cakes, fruit, gefilte fish, taglach, almonds, raisins, sweets, bottles of brandy, whisky, vishnik, lemonade and kola. The room was crowded with female cousins and assorted neighbours who had come to give the bride a happy send off. Everyone was talking at the top of her voice and helping themselves to the abundant food and drink available. We children were greeted with a salvo of 'Oohs and Ahs'. Our cheeks were pinched and hot wet kisses planted on us from all sides. Then the bride, fully decked out in all her finery, emerged from the bedroom carrying her long train in her arms like a cloud of spun sugar. The air grew thick with mazeltovs and tearful good wishes. During the tumult, my sister and I were presented with ribbon-covered shepherd's crooks supporting bouquets of flowers which we were instructed to hold in our free hands. Soon it was time to leave for the synagogue in Great Philpot Street. Without mishap we entered the waiting carriage, passing through a guard of honour spontaneously assembled by my aunt's immediate neighbours. From the carriage I could see people waving to us from their windows facing the street.

When we reached the synagogue, my sister and I were given final advice and instructions by Mother, who put the train in our hands and told us to hold on at all costs. Then stepping out boldly, we passed through the pillared portals of the entrance into the noisy interior where the chuppa, erected in front of the Ark, stood waiting to receive the bride. The canopy was of blue velvet with goldwire decoration. A Hebrew phrase was worked into the floral motif, and the structure, supported at each corner by slender poles of brass-capped wood, looked like a magic flying carpet. The ceremony commenced immediately, the cantor singing the traditional blessings with stylish technique and joy. The wine was sipped, the ring consecrated and placed on my aunt's finger, and the bridegroom stamped on a wine glass to the vociferous cries of mazeltov and the audible weeping of my mother and the groom's female family. My sister and I had an attack of the giggles, and I wanted to wee wee rather urgently.

We left the synagogue in procession and according to protocol. Three horse-drawn carriages were lined up to operate a shuttle service bringing the guests to the banqueting hall where breakfast was scheduled at 2 pm. Until then, drinks and snacks were freely available. At two o'clock, the meal began, consisting of chopped liver for starters, lockshen soup, fried

sole, giblet pie, roast chicken and stuffed neck, almond pudding, compote
and cups of acrid black coffee. Drinks were served throughout the meal,
ranging from whisky, brandy, hocks and kosher wines, to exotic liqueurs.
Throughout the meal an orchestra vied with the ear-splitting conversation

and boisterous good humour, and only received a hearing when the violin sobbed out one of the more sentimental ballads of the day. This was always good for a round of applause, and a tear or two shed into a wine cup.

After 'breakfast', the guests went home to sleep it off and change into evening wear for the Dinner and Ball to come. Around six o'clock they would return to the hall, where tea and pastries were served immediately at small tables dotted round the perimeter.

Meanwhile, the caterer and his staff had been busy. The tables in the centre of the floor were set out in sprigs and laid for dinner. They made a pretty picture dressed in flowers and simlox trailing leaves which were attached to golden hooded sticks placed between the tables. Each table had its own centrepiece of a large silver bowl containing carefully prepared pyramids of fruit in season. Also resplendently tall silver candelabra whose serpentine coils carried large red candles that dripped red wax onto the cloth like drops of blood.

From its special niche, the orchestra, Flaum's, with Moishe the Trumpeter, kept up a steady barrier of noise which was broken by the conversation of the assembled guests. When I grew tired during the evening, mother would put me down to nap near the orchestra, where I was allowed to tap the hanging pipes or cymbals before surrendering to sleep covered by a pile of overcoats. Several other children would eventually succumb to ennui and be laid alongside, so that we looked like an illustration by Gustave Doré depicting a slum workhouse. Here and there around the hall, card players were starting up games of solo and klobiosh that would go on for the rest of the evening, only stopping for meals.

At eight o'clock dinner was announced, and the guests seated themselves in their allotted places ready to face up to whatever the perspiring waiters would place before them. With a flourish of his baton, the orchestra leader launched his men into the lively strains of 'Chosen Calla Mazeltov', which was accompanied by the tapping of forks on wine glasses by the guests assembled. In the midst of this tumult, the bride and groom in full regalia made a splendid entrance. Here again my sister and I were pressed into service holding on to our aunt's train for dear life. This was to be our penultimate appearance. Only the posing for photographs remained, and Suss of Whitechapel was already setting up the camera and backdrop of palms and pillars in an adjoining room.

The waiters served the hors d'oeuvres and from that moment on were occupied for the next two hours serving dish after dish of glorious food. There was lockshen soup and meatballs ladled onto the plates from splendid silver tureens. Then veal cutlets followed with trimmings of this and that; sorbet ice; roast duck or chicken in gargantuan portions with attendant potatoes and peas; asparagus; fruits; coffee and liqueurs. Stays were surreptitiously unhooked and trouser waistbands unbuttoned to allow for the formidable expansion. The chatter at table was ear-splitting and it was with great difficulty that the guests were brought to order for grace after meals which was intoned by the bridegroom's father. The sing-song responses and the final blessing on the wine brought the great banquet to an end.

Now various members of each family stood up and delivered themselves of long, boring and mercifully inaudible speeches, extolling the merits of both the bride and groom. Tears were shed as one mentioned a loved one long since dead; tears were shed when another mentioned relatives still in Russia enduring the hardships of the recent Revolution. An argument broke out at one table between the Bolsheviks and the Mensheviks. Old people, overcome by the unaccustomed huge helpings of food and wine, were snoring peacefully in their seats oblivious to the sturm and drang around them. Every guest was presented with a paper fan and small engagement book to which was attached a tiny pencil dangling at the end of a silk cord. Each page was ruled up to take the name of a prospective partner and the dance for which he or she had engaged themselves. Already some of the 'fast' ones in the company were soliciting partners quite openly and without shame.

When the final speech and final toast had been made, the guests were invited to return to the small tables round the hall where the interrupted card games were resumed. Meanwhile, the waiters roamed the hall serving halved apples, oranges, peeled bananas, pineapple rings and sweets. For the younger generation, the indefatigable orchestra kept up a steady flow of dance music ranging from the Viennese waltz to the Russian kezutski. The noise became three-dimensional. Suddenly a roll on the drums and the tinny resonance of the cymbal produced a pocket of silence during which the maestro announced in Yiddish that the photographer was now ready to operate at the further end of the hall. Here a series of steps had been erected so that the guests could stand in rows yet not osbcure the person behind. After a lot of argument as to who should stand where and next to whom, the group finally came to rest. My sister and I were draped each side of the bride and groom, our crooks with the floral decorations artistically arranged to best advantage. The rest of the children were set out on the polished parquet of the floor and asked to watch the birdie. The camera looking like a three-legged ostrich, stood facing us, the photographer under his velvet cloth twiddling the focusing mechanism. He emerged and picked up the flash apparatus which he primed and held over his head. This was the moment of truth. 'Everybody keep still', he shouted in Yiddish. He removed the lens cap and fired the magnesium, which flared up in a proverbial flash. A bit more fiddling with the plate carrier, and another negative was exposed. When this was concluded, the guests drifted back to their tables and dancing, whilst the camera immortalised the stars of the evening's drama. The bride and groom; the bride, groom and attendants; the parents of the groom and his brother and sister; the bride's cousins, uncles, aunts, sister and in-laws. Shot after shot, plate after plate was exposed, to be delivered mounted on board and suitable for framing at some time within a week or so of the ordering.

By midnight, the main sprig of tables had been relaid for another sit-down meal consisting of matzas, butter, strudels, jellies, blancmanges, cheeses, patisserie and lashings of tea. By now, the men had been sorted out from the boys. It was a fraction of the original number that actually came to the tables to partake of the light refreshment. The joie de vivre of the early evening had somehow lost itself in a surfeit of food and indigestion.

The caterer was preparing his account at one of the spare tables, carefully watched by the unterfuehrers. The cost of the evening worked out at about 27s. 6d. a couple. This was inclusive. Before taking on the job, the caterer had gone over the proposed guest list with the host of the affair in order to ascertain the probable tips likely to accrue during the evening. If the prognosis had been poor, the caterer would not have undertaken the job. He actually depended on the tips for his profit. The cook and waiters did their own soliciting for alms as the guests departed at the end of the evening. This was accepted by all concerned and the obligation religiously adhered to.

The function usually terminated in the early hours of the morning. I never saw it through, having slept alongside the bandstand until I was lifted up onto my father's shoulder and carried home to bed, still clutching my beribboned shepherd's crook and garland of wilting flowers.

A Man Already

From the age of eight or nine, sons of the natives were made aware of the approach of barmitzvah. The daily visits to Chedar or Hebrew classes where with blood, sweat and tears, the Rabbi hammered away at his oft unyielding material in an endeavour to impart the basics of religion, multiplied as the years passed by. With their passing, the reluctant student suddenly found himself in barmitzvah class. Here, having ascertained the relevant portion of the Torah coincident with his thirteenth birthday, work would begin in earnest. Together with several of his comrades, he would repeat and repeat the blessings, maftir and haftorah destined to be his lot. He was also expected to learn a brief but sentimental speech, usually composed by his Rabbi, to declaim at the celebratory party following his synagogue debut. This cliché-riddled oration was repeated in Yiddish, English and Hebrew, and was designed to bring approbation to the Rabbi and tears to the eyes of the boy's loving mother. When the day arrived, it was the thought of the presents he would receive that sustained the lad in his ordeal.

*   *   *

'Get up,' said my mother, 'It will soon be time to go to shool.' I woke up and suddenly realised that today was my barmitzvah. A new blue serge suit with my first pair of long trousers was hanging from the gas bracket on the wall. A pair of glacé kid shoes, also new, reposed under the chair by my bed. This was it. The great day! I dressed myself carefully, then breakfasted on a piece of cholla which stuck in my throat, and washed it down with a cup of tea. By now my parents and sisters were decked out in their yomtov best, ready for the mile walk to our synagogue. We set out under a barrage of mazeltovs fired by neighbours who were also members of the congregation.

In a dingy side street off Brick Lane, the synagogue was already filling up with regulars. The noise as we entered was terrific. Also the smell of camphor balls, snuff, and old books. Mother and sister kissed me, then walked up the stairs to the 'U'-shaped women's gallery. My father and I took our usual places behind the bimah. Here I underwent an ordeal of cheek-pinching and head-patting until the service started. All too soon it was time for the sacred scrolls to be taken from the ark for the reading of the week's sidra. As the barmitzvah's sire, my father was privileged to stand by the reader's desk throughout the ceremony, no doubt in readiness to support me in my time of need. Above the incessant hum of conversation, I suddenly heard my Hebrew name called and nervously made my way towards the bimah. The shammis began to slap his bible vigorously and called for silence and respect for the barmitzvah boy.

As the noise subsided, in a faltering voice I began singing the blessing. Soon I was oblivious of the surroundings and, confident in my ability to perform the ceremony, sang loud and clear, revelling in the occasion. The Torah was removed and a chumash set for the haftorah. On the crest of the wave I sang on, hitching my tallis and swaying to and fro like a dervish, until the last response to the final blessing indicated that it was all over. From the men came cries of 'shecoiach' and from the gallery a shower of almonds and raisins, with which the women had been primed for this purpose by my mother. Kids scrambled at my feet snatching up the fruit that had escaped being trodden into the carpet. Still elated, I walked towards the gallery steps, shaking hands with all and sundry en route. Upstairs my mother, still in tears, kissed and hugged me, looking up from time to time at her surrounding companions to say, 'It's mine son, a barmitzvah boy already'. Then the rest of the women kissed and cried over me. I returned to my seat for the conclusion of the Sabbath service which came as an anti-climax after the foregoing excitement.

When it was over, about thirty people walked home with us to celebrate Kiddush. The results of the feverish preparations in the kitchen on the previous day were spread on the table. Gefilte fish balls, fried fish balls, herring (chopped), herring (pickled), herring (schmaltz), cucumbers, yeastcake, gingercake, the whole dwarfed by an enormous cholla specially baked for the occasion. My father intoned the Kiddush, blessing the Sabbath wine and bread. Wine and whisky were dispensed and drunk to my long life and health. My cheeks were pinched, my back slapped and when I was suitably softened up, the kissing started again in order of seniority. First my mother, then my aunts, cousins, landsleit, and the woman next door. By now, reaction had set in. I grew hot and cold and hot again. My Rabbi, who had been hovering in the background, suddenly seized my arm and in an alcoholic whisper said 'Make the first speech'. Cries of 'Quiet' and 'Shuddup a minute' slowly abated to comparative silence. A shaky chair was provided, and I was helped to stand on it. Our relatives and guests, glasses in hand, looked up at me lovingly.

'My beloved parents, sisters, relatives, rabbi and friends, today I am a man.' My voice droned on repeating parrot-wise, in Yiddish, the words I had committed to heart many weeks ago. I thanked my parents for the good Jewish upbringing they had given me, together with their love. I thanked my Rabbi for teaching me the ways of godliness despite my lack of enthusiasm (pause for laughter while he explained that he was the author of my witty oration), and finally I thanked my relatives and friends for joining me on this great and important day in the life of a Jewish boy. I then burst into tears.

The party proper took place the following day. The front room of our flat was miraculously cleared of all unnecessary furniture and a table improvised, which ran the length of the room. Long planks of wood resting on kitchen chairs made up the seating arrangements. Immediately after our makeshift breakfast, my mother and two aunts, specially co-opted, retired to the kitchen where they roasted, boiled and baked the foodstuffs for the evening feast. At seven o'clock the guests began trickling in; by seven-thirty the trickle became an avalanche. My mother and father, dressed to kill, greeted them at the top of the stairs. I was standing by to receive the gifts that were showered on me in a series of tearful hugs, kisses and good wishes. From time to time I would dart into the bedroom and quickly tear open the packages to examine the goods to date. Swan fountain pens with eyedrop fillers (3), gold chain (1), silver chain (1), cigarette case (silver), match box container (silver), portable toilet set encased in leather (1), a gold tie pin, pentateuchs (5 sets), prayer book (heavily ornamented in red plush, silver filigree and ivory), an Ingersoll wristwatch with a caged protector that obscured the dial, a ping-pong set, etcetera.

By eight o'clock all the guests had arrived and were seated round the table ready for action. My Rabbi, in the place of honour at the top end, quickly pronounced the blessing over bread and we were under way. For two hours the feasting continued. Chopped liver, soups with lokshen, craplech and knoedel; chicken, meats, stuffed neck, stuffed cabbage, tzimas, puddings, pies, strudel, stewed apple, compote and finally, glasses of lemon tea, brandy, whisky and home-made cherry brandy. The noise was boisterous and uninhibited, and the room's temperature like that of a Turkish bath. Perspiration bedewed each forehead like drops of rain on a window pane.

My Rabbi, now slightly the worse for drink, gabbled the Grace after meals joined by the guests in the sing-song responses. Then a few sharp thumps on the table and the noise abated. It was now my turn to entertain the assembly—first with a trio of identical speeches in Yiddish, Hebrew and English which produced a flood of tears from my mother, aunts, cousins and our nearest neighbour who lived in the flat below. Then with a specially rehearsed rendering of Dvorak's Humoresque on the violin, which produced another flood of tears from the music-lovers present. Having concluded my part of the ceremonial, I was told to go to the kitchen where I assisted with the washing up until my fingers, wrinkled by the coarse washing soda water softener, looked like elongated walnuts.

Party Peace

At 11 o'clock in the morning of November 11th 1918, The Great War to end all wars came to a negotiated end. It cost ten million lives, and changed the frontiers of thirty countries. Fathers and sons began to trickle home from far away places carrying their battle-stained kitbags behind them. They had awesome tales to tell of Verdun, the Marne, Ypres, Mesopotamia and Salonica. They recalled the horror of screaming shells and blistering poison gasses that drifted into the trenches on a prevailing wind and left a residue of blindness and coughed-up lung tissue in their wake. We children listened in open-mouthed wonder, tried on their shrapnel-scarred steel helmets, and asked them for cigarette cards or war souvenirs. The soldiers were tough, squat men, their legs puttee-bound like Egyptian mummies, their badges and buttons Brasso polished to rival the sun. There were Canadians, Yanks and Anzacs in bush hats, looking for Sheilas in the quarter, and finding them. Then arm in arm to the *Virginia Planter* or the *Columbia Arms*, where girls in cloche hats and short skirts, under which bells on their garters tinkled mysteriously as they walked, drank pints of beer or glasses of port.

In school, the Allied victory was celebrated by singing 'God save the King,' and an award of a bronze Peace medal and a white china beaker sporting a coloured transfer of George V and Queen Mary on its side. All over the quarter, senior citizens organised celebratory street parties where food and entertainment were generously provided by voluntary subscription. We soon forgot the nightmare Zeppelin raids that forced us to seek safety under the protective arches of the Great Eastern Railway horse depot opposite the Olympia theatre in Shoreditch, or the sneak daylight raids of Gothas that came out of the clouds to drop their bombs before a policeman's whistle could signal the raid and the natives go to ground. It was parties, parties everywhere, and knees up Mother Brown.

★   ★   ★

'Put on a clean shirt and comb the hair,' said my mother to me. It was August 1919 and a Peace party was being prepared round the corner in Gossett Street. The local churches and mission halls provided trestle tables and chairs, which were set up in the middle of the roadway between Newling Street at one end and Brick Lane at the other. All the lamp-posts

along the route were decorated with bunting, and most of the tenement windows facing the street sported Union Jacks and portraits of the King and Queen wearing their coronation regalia. The tables were placed end to end and covered with white cloths or patched bed sheets. Aspidistras, geraniums and spiky palms in neat red pots were used as decoration. Plates of paste and cheese sandwiches, rock cakes, scones and slabs of lard cake were heaped up everywhere. There were jellies and brick hard ice cream portions between wafers.

Weak tea was brewed up in urns in the church hall, and for those who preferred cold drinks there was lemonade made up of crystals dissolved in a huge galvanised zinc bath.

My hair was parted down the centre and smarmed onto my scalp like a hirsute swimming cap. I was given a tin mug for drinking out of and a penny contribution towards the party expenses. Mrs Lindsay, the local policeman's wife, was in charge of the Gibraltar Walk contingent and she helped sort out the seating arrangements. It was summer at the time and we were blessed with a cloudless sky and a warm day. At 3.30 pm, together with about 150 other children, I was seated at the festive table waiting for the word 'go'.

First we sang songs led by a man at the piano on a raised dais outside the church hall from which source it had no doubt been acquired. This was a great novelty to see a piano in the street where the barrel organ and cornet had right of way. We sang 'Daisy, Daisy' and 'Keep the home fires burning', 'Ma, she's making eyes at me' and finished with 'Rule Britannia' and a bit of flag waving. It was great fun sitting in the street. All the side turnings were blocked to traffic; painted notices informed would-be intruders that a street party was in progress. There were soldiers in khaki and sailors in blue with bell-bottom trousers, who passed the jellies and ice-cream or served the tea. Some were wounded and on convalescent leave, easily recognisable by their light blue suits, white shirts and red ties. Here and there a one-armed man would lend a hand, his empty sleeve pinned up to the shoulder; or a one-legged cripple swinging along on crutches, his shoulders hunched up with the effort. Gunners, infantrymen, engineers and a couple of VAD's seemed to be doing all the chores. We sang more songs and several of the children were sick with overeating and too much excitement. They were taken into the mission hall for first aid and a sponge down.

Meanwhile, the piano thumped away into a 'Knees-up' which was a signal for the adult spectators to break into the traditional Mittel-East dance. The noise was terrific. When both the pianist and dancers were exhausted, one of the organisers sprang onto the platform and ordered us to leave the tables and form a long orderly queue. Then one by one we were led into the mission hall and presented with a paper bag containing a bar of chocolate, caramels, a sherbet dab and a licorice laced gob-stopper. We left the building by a rear exit into Virginia Road. Still clutching my tin mug and the bag of goodies, I made my way back home to Gibraltar Walk where my Mother told me not to eat any of my gift sweets until after supper.

The Spoken Word

The natives spoke in a motley of tongues. Each waking day, the polyglot of sound between families and neighbours erupted in gutteral Yiddish, authoritative Russian, spluttering Dutch or the cut and thrust of Polish. My parents were Russian and spoke to each other in the language of the Czars. My sister and I, born in the native quarter, were slowly absorbing the intricacies of English grammar and speech, which we delivered with cockney intonation and certainty. Our common means of communication was Yiddish. Despite heavy economic pressures, my parents found time to learn to speak and read English after a fashion. The full meaning of many of the phrases they used was often misunderstood and most certainly misheard. Nevertheless, communication in the idiom of their adopted country was soon possible.

★   ★   ★

One Friday evening, my mother said to me, 'You can stay up late tonight. After supper, we are going to Uncle Barnet.' This was a most unusual occurrence since visiting on the Sabbath eve was strictly de trop in the Mittel East. However, since my uncle and aunt lived must around the corner, it imposed no physical hardship on my parents, nor did it cause them to commit a sin by riding in a bus or tram.

When we arrived at Uncle Barnet's house, he was already entertaining several other relatives and landsleit. My sister and I were soundly kissed by the assembly, loaded up with chunks of crumbly yeast cake, sweets and fruit, and then told to play with our cousin 'Little Harry' and his toys. The adults were served with whisky or brandy as they conversed in ear-splitting Yiddish or Russian. Their inhibitions lowered by a drink or two, some of the guests began to speak in English. My aunt had been to the Lane to buy some remblings (remnants). She was making a new dress for her sister-in-law to be. Another chance remark from a landsman elicited the information that his boss, a wealthy furrier, had just moved to a big house in Stamford Hill which had a lovely conservative (conservatory) full of flowers.

Most of the people present that night were members of the Workers' Circle, a sort of club for immigrants, where politics, music and other cultural activities added a little colour to the drabness of their lives. A recent series of lectures became the topic of conversation. My mother, who had attended most of them, said how interesting it was to learn about Mrs Pankhurst and the Selfridgettes. On domestic issues, clodovo-lime (Chloride of lime) was recommended to keep the drains clean, as was quckleroats (Quaker Oats) for breakfast. Comment was also passed on the Salmation Army, whose Sunday afternoon Evangelism accompanied by a big brass band, shattered the post-lunch siesta of the natives. The talk turned to walks in the neighbourhood of Tareel Bridtz (Tower Bridge), or in the West End by Mummel Arch (Marble Arch). A popular place for coffee was in the Lyons Corner House opposite Charry and Cross Station (Charing Cross Station).

Most of these conversations were conducted mainly in Yiddish, with the odd English word or two breaking through like a rash of measles. We youngsters suffered from this strange lingual montage, accepting it as a normal mode of speech.

A common sight in the Mittel East was that of a small child, standing in the middle of the roadway, looking up at a window of the tenement in front of him. Suddenly his face would grow red with the effort of screaming at the top of his voice.

'Mum. Cut me off, schmeer me on and chuck me down!' This would be followed by the appearance of the child's mother, who would angrily hurl down a small newsprint-wrapped parcel which, when opened by her demanding offspring, brought to view a large slice of brown bread, liberally spread with chicken fat and gribenes.

I Wish
You Better

'Remain by me well,' was a standard greeting in fear of sickness that brought in its wake an untold misery of endless hours spent in the Out-patients of the local hospital or calling in the doctor with the prospect of bills to pay. At least the hospital was free. Patients would be herded together on long polished benches like travellers waiting for their trains at the terminus. Here they hoped to see the doctor or a matron. The noise was overpowering. Babies cried, children screamed, already frightened by the strange sight of mysterious trolleys covered by red blankets and the sound of tinkling instruments coming from the casualty department. Worst of all was the nervous incessant chatter of the mums that swept over everything like the sea of an incoming tide over the sand.

As you entered the hospital, your name, address and other pertinent facts were recorded on a card by the Almoner. Also on the card was the back and unsexed front outline of a human body. If you had stomach ache, a cross would be made on the abdominal region of the drawing. This was a diagnostic hint to the doctor when the time came for consultation. The woman at the desk would direct you to a seat in the waiting area where you sat until called to the surgery.

From time to time, in response to their names, a family group would detach itself from the mass and disappear behind a screen where the doctor on duty sat, stethoscope at the ready, to deal with whatever ailment the symptoms indicated. There were other screens in the same room from behind which moans and groans filtered into the carbolic reeking atmosphere. Occasionally a glimpse of a naked body would flash into view as a wayward child moved the curtains. This would produce an hysterical cry (in Yiddish) of embarrassment and outrage from the patient until a reassuring gesture from the nurse brought the noise down to its normal headaching level.

Despite the continual noise and distraction, the doctor would make a fair diagnosis and write a prescription which was handed in to the hospital dispensary. Here again the waiting was tedious, the children fighting and scrambling to ride the large wooden rocking horse placed in this area by the well-meaning but short-sighted authorities. Tea, buns, and sandwiches were available at low prices from the coffee-stall type canteen. Here again the female patients exchanged intimate details about their respective ills and experiences with the doctor, until one's name was called from the dispensary where one collected a bottle of coloured liquid or an assortment of pills rattling in a varnished red cardboard container.

For natives who were prepared to pay rather than undergo the hurly burly of the hospital, there were several doctors in the quarter who were revered by their satisfied patients. We patronised a Dr Rogers whose waiting room, surgery-cum-dispensary were within easy walking distance in Church Street diagonally opposite Haltrecht's haberdashery store in Bethnal Green Road and immediately opposite the Ladies and Gents convenience on the corner. Nearby, Fox the chemist not only supplied prescribed specifics but was the stockist and purveyor of the folksy remedies beloved by the immigrant population.

During winter, when ills and chills were rife, we children were rubbed with tallow, dosed with a concoction of honey and forced to wear a perforated camphor locket round our necks which impregnated the air around us, ostensibly to ward off the maladies of the moment. We were also subjected to lavings of eucalyptus oil, wintergreen ointment and other sundry medicants that healed or soothed or cauterised.

Dr Rogers was a great favourite with the children. His consulting room was full of bric-a-brac collected during a sojourn in India and he would talk about them whilst tapping or prodding the source of the trouble. Heavy mahogany glass fronted cases filled with leather-bound medical books covered three walls of the room, and an assortment of syringes, enemas, rubber tubing and test tubes reposed on a glass-topped trolley at his elbow. In place of honour above the consulting desk was a live barn owl on a perch in its cage. It never moved or blinked an eye and to this day I believe it was stuffed. On this same desk was a cut glass brass-bound inkstand which shared the crowded space with an old stethoscope and a beaker containing several wooden spatulas and another holding a clinical thermometer immersed in an opaque disinfectant.

During winter, a coke fire burned in the grate so that undressing for examination was not an unpleasant experience. The only heavily curtained window at the further end of the room shed its feeble light on the black American cloth-covered couch from the frayed corners of which the horse hair emerged like fire from a dragon's nostrils.

Dr Rogers wore pince-nez and sported a bushy square-cut beard which covered most of his Gladstone collar and the tie held in place by a diamond pin. He was a kindly sympathetic soul and was loved and admired by all his patients. The response, 'Dr Rogers said so', was enough to bring any argument to an end.

The native quarter was also served by several Mission hospitals, the Mildmay at the bottom end of Virginia Road, being our nearest. Here medicine was dispensed on a religious exchange basis. You sang a hymn or two, muttered a few amens after the prayers recited by a nun on bended knees and before you could say St Peter, you saw the doctor and came out of the place clutching the inevitable bottle of linctus or embrocation.

Different hospitals were recognised by the indigent population as being better at curing certain illnesses whilst falling down on others. Already the cry of 'Is he a specialist?' was making itself manifest. The services of Dr Schroeder of the German Hospital were legendary.

We also used the Queen Mary's Hospital for Children in Hackney Road at the corner of Goldsmith Row where my friend Joe Glassman lived. In summer, the 'in-patients' were wheeled out of the wards into the comparative fresh air of the open balconies facing the street. When my sister was rushed to this hospital with a bad attack of colic brought on by her eating a bag full of unripe cherries and kept in for a week, the whole family would take a walk to the hospital every evening and wave to her from the pavement in front of the main entrance. On our way home my mother would cry.

On the Bridge at Midnight

Amusement was cheap in price and invariably habit-forming. On Saturday nights natives went to the cinema (locally) or the theatre (West End). Saturday evenings were also club-time for both adults and their young. Parents would go off to the Workers' Circle in Great Alie Street where over a game of chess (intellectual), draughts (low-brow), or cards (family), the time would pass pleasantly and workaday cares drowned in innumerable glasses of lemon tea. The teenagers had their own way of life, bound by the rules and customs of the quarter. Their days were measured in units of schooltime and homework, leaving little to spare for leisure. It was after the Friday night kindling of the Sabbath candles and the termination of the evening meal that followed that the young came into their own. With the prospect of a weekend's freedom from school, the strain and anxiety of keeping up with Latin, maths, history, English and geography was packed away with the relevant lexicons in the satchels they carried to school. This was the hour for the weekly promenade to the Tower Bridge.

★   ★   ★

'If you are going for a walk now,' said my mother, 'put on the overcoat.' It was Friday night. The Sabbath meal had long since been eaten and the white starched table cloth cleared of all the debris. Now the three brass candlesticks with their steady burning candles shared the space with an ornamental fruit-bowl topped up with apples and oranges in readiness for the enjoyment of any visitor that might drop in unexpectedly. My father, gently moving to and fro in his rocking chair, was already immersed in the *Jewish Express*. He took an occasional nip from the brandy glass at his elbow. My mother would close the kitchen door behind me, but not before delivering a final reminder that I was not to come home late. Afterwards she would seat herself at the table to read the current copy of *Peg's Paper*. This was her self-conducted English lesson of the week.

In the street below my friends would be waiting. After a bit of good-natured horseplay, we would start the traditional trek to the Bridge. Bethnal Green was a long way from our rendezvous and we had several calls to make en route to pick up stragglers who were members of our particular group. Through the dingy gas-lit streets of the native quarter, we would sing and joke our way, delighting in our freedom from the nightly stint of homework and the cares to be faced in the morning. Down Brick Lane, with its shuttered shop fronts now strangely silent and forlorn, without the babble of womenfolk which normally animated the scene. Across Bethnal Green Road and down the Lane, usually alive with the cries of fish and fruit vendors who displayed their wares in the light of hissing naphtha flares. Now the place was silent and empty. Just a stray cat sniffing at an unswept fish head in the gutter reminded us that here was the market-place of our quarter. We ambled along, making plans for the morrow. Was there enough money available for a visit to a West End theatre, or should we go to the cinema, a much less expensive prospect? Soon we were under the railway arch where our voices, purposely raised, echoed joyfully from the soot-grimed roof. On down the road past the smell of the brewery cellars that lined each side of the malty way. Into Osborne Street, where the Whitechapel pavements were aswarm with friends and acquaintances also on the evening's promenade. Several of them attached themselves to our caravanserai. Now about fifteen strong, we headed for Leman Street where the public houses were doing a roaring business. At the bottom end of Leman Street we turned right towards Tower Hill, with the Mint a brooding silhouette in the darkness.

We were now practically at journey's end. The skeletal outlines of the Bridge rose before us, and we rushed helter skelter across the road to take up positions with one foot either side of the movable sections of the bridge. When a car passed over this spot, the structure would swing separately and a most pleasant sensation passed up through one's shoes to the top of one's head. When this activity palled, we leaned over the balustrades and spat into the water below. This was a particularly enjoyable pastime, especially when a barge floated by. The tarpaulin decks of the unsuspecting craft would be dominoed with specks of saliva.

We crossed and recrossed the track, clambering up into the ironwork decorations that provided agreeable footholds. We searched out ships at anchor in the darkness and cried out the strange foreign-sounding names with exaggerated accents. From far away places in our geography books, these vessels came into the River Thames, with fruits, furniture, wools and cottons, so that we could eat and clothe ourselves.

After a while, the excitement would die down and we reassembled for the return to the quarter. Here again custom decreed that we wander back on the Tower side, pacing the perimeter of the wide and empty moat that looked like a school playground in the gloom, the grey stones of the Tower walls with their slotted bowmen's windows forming an eerie background to our perambulations. Tired but happy, we retraced our steps to the native quarter, avoiding the drunks who staggered across our path with alarming frequency. At intervals, the group would dwindle as we reached somebody's home. Loud cries of 'See you tomorrow' or just 'Goodnight' punctuated our promenade until the final 'Cheerio' when the last couple parted company in the now silent quarter.

Apprentice

For the non-academic offspring the need to work for a livelihood was pressing. Unlike their clever colleagues who were matriculation orientated with a future at university in mind, they were under pressure to contribute to the family income where the emphasis was on the immediate present. Leaving school at fourteen years of age and inadequately equipped to take up appointments in commerce, the majority entered industry to learn the skills of cabinet-making, upholstery or tailoring. Usually they worked for the same firms as did their fathers where under the parental eye, they quickly developed into craftsmen. It was unusual for a son to 'break away' from the accepted tradition, and in so doing cause a great deal of heart-searching and head shaking in the family advisory circle.

★　　★　　★

'What for a black year is Photo-engraving?' my mother asked me as I put on my overcoat in readiness to leave for work. The previous week I had signed indentures that bound me for five years apprenticeship to the Arc Engraving Company, situated in a narrow avenue off Fleet Street. My Uncle Jack who was a foreman printer at Waterlows had advised my parents to let me enter the process engraving field instead of the hurly burly of cabinet-making, with its ever increasing seasonal slack periods. With the aid of a Trade Scholarship, I had left my Central school at fourteen years of age to attend the LCC School of Photo Engraving and Lithography, where the theory and chemistry of the trade I was to adopt was made explicit. At sixteen I was ready to be apprenticed since the Union did not encourage the employment of unindentured operatives.

Every morning I got up at six o'clock, washed, dressed and breakfasted in readiness to catch the seven o'clock workman's bus to Fleet Street from the stop in front of Shoreditch Church, with my lunch of cheese platzels in a butter stained bag firmly gripped in my hand. On arriving at my destination, I would run up the forty stairs or more leading to the clock into which every employee had to insert his own named card and record the time of his arrival. It was invariably eight o'clock when I got to work, punctuality being encouraged by the loss of wages incurred at a minute after ten past the hour. My daily attendance was from 8 am to 6 pm with an hour off for lunch and a ten minute break both morning and afternoon. I also worked a halfday every alternate Saturday. For this I received 17s. 6d. per week, plus overtime at Union rates and less Union dues.

My job for the first year of my apprenticeship consisted of sweeping up a room the size of a medium dance hall, oiling inadequately insulated machinery which, on contact, would practically prostrate me with electric shock. I made tea twice a day for the three journeymen who were to teach me the job. I also ran all errands for them, including the daily purchase of hot meals at a local public house and every edition of the racing edition of the *Star*.

Our workshop was the top floor of an old stonefaced building with 125 steep wooden stairs leading up to it. During the day I walked up and down them about eight times. Because corrosive chemicals were used in the engraving process, I would wear my father's cast-off trousers over my own and protect my shirt with his old waistcoats. I was always afraid that one of my current girl friends would see me looking like an animated scarecrow when on errands in the street, so I usually detoured through the conveniently placed courts and alleyways that burrow through Fleet Street.

The midday lunches, purchased at the *Two Brewers* hostelry in Shoe Lane, were stacked in special carriers rather like Victorian portable cake stands, each plate of meat and two veg. being covered by a metal dome on which the plate above rested. The other apprentices in the firm engaged on similar chores would congregate at a counter inside the street door entrance, uncover the food and help themselves to chips, sausages, slices of beef or vegetables. Apart from satisfying one's hunger, this meant a saving of several shillings a week on food. As a kosher-conditioned native of the Mittel East, I stuck to my cheese platzels and raw fruit, having explained my reluctance to partake on religious rather than ethical grounds.

The three men who were my instructors treated me with great consideration, even encouraging the talent I was beginning to show as an artist. Although the job we did was known as engraving, the process

was mechanically applied. The end product of blocks for printing in newspapers and magazines required no artistic training. One of the trio was an inveterate and compulsive gambler, losing most of his weekly pay packet at cards or horse racing.

After eating lunch, a trestle table would be set up near the fireplace and the 'brag' school would be in session until the shop steward, or Father of the Chapel as he was called in the print world (the name stemming from the time of Caxton, who set up his first printing press in the crypt of a chapel), would come in, watch in hand, calling 'time's up' until the last round was played out. The wall over the fireplace was covered in chalk graffiti stating 'Tom owes me 2s.', or 'Jim to pay 3s. 6d.', the date of each debt carefully inscribed by the sum.

Each Friday it was part of my job to make a list of who owed what to whom, and with the debtor's pay packet in hand, make the necessary restitution. This was quite a lucrative undertaking for me. Most of those repaid would give me a sixpence for my trouble as did the debtor for doing the rounds. My weekend entertainment depended on these 'extras', and out of the evils of gambling I attended many a West End theatre or cinema, sometimes with a girl in tow.

After two years of Union-controlled charring, in the intervals between which I was familiarised with the techniques of the craft until I could be trusted to carry out a job without supervision. My foreman, a round-shouldered bald-headed Welshman who was never seen without a hand-rolled cigarette stuck to his lower lip and open at the burning end like the horn of an old time gramophone, taught me all the tricks of the trade. This was a feather in my cap, since he was known throughout the pro-fession as a beer-swilling misanthrope. I was still obliged to run errands, make tea, etc., but there was a perceptible difference in their attitude toward me. The men were already accepting me as a fully-fledged crafts-man. Even the general manager, an Austrian called Otto, who used to rage and swear at the drop of a Tyrolean hat, for the performance of which he deserved a tribute, since at heart he was the kindliest of men and a good friend to boot, jealously guarding the good name and honour of every employee—even he would pause in mid-anger to compliment me on a job.

In all, I spent five years in the firm, at the end of which I could regard myself as an expert engraver. At noon of the day I turned twenty-one years of age, I was ceremoniously 'banged 'out of my apprenticeship. The father of the Chapel began to bang on a tin with a stick. Soon all the firm were beating tins, metal plates and enamel mugs. In the midst of this pandemonium, I walked silently through each department and down the stairs into the street. Symbolically, I was no longer an apprentice. I had been traditionally drummed out and could call myself a journeyman with increase of pay commensurate with my new standing.

At one o'clock, I returned to the firm's boardroom, where all the direc-tors, managers, foremen, and my uncle (standing in for my father who couldn't get away from work for the occasion) awaited my arrival, glasses of whisky in hand ready to drink my health and future. One year later I was sacked and joined the ranks of the unemployed.

Nation Shall Speak to Nation

In my sector of the Mittel East, culture was strictly for the rich. Only the left-wing intelligentsia working class would get together in their Sunday socialist clubs for an educational hour or so, listening to piano recitals or an edifying lecture on some political theme, usually delivered in Yiddish. Later, with the advent of radio, it became possible for anyone to purchase an inexpensive wireless set and, in the discomfort of his own home, listen to good music and folksy lectures, and be up-to-the-minute with world news. The radio soon became a status symbol and many an early valve set with its symbiotic swan-necked loud-speaker would be proudly displayed in the front-room window at street level, displacing the ubiquitous aspidistra that had ruled this particular roost from time immemorial.

★ ★ ★

One Sunday after dinner my mother said to me, 'Father has bought a wireless'. I was overjoyed at the prospect, and after the table was cleared and the washing up done, my father produced the set. It was a twelve inch square of polished mahogany with a neat moulding round the edges. On this, a wire-wound cylinder about ten inches long and five in diameter, was firmly mounted. Two brass rods with sliding plungers completed the tube assembly. Screw terminals marked 'Earth', 'Aerial', and 'Headphones' were distributed on the base, together with a small cup containing a Hertzite crystal over which a cat's-whisker armature trembled. With tremendous enthusiasm we erected a twenty two yard aerial around the room, earthed the set to the kitchen tap and with our N & K earphones firmly fixed over our ears, plunged into the ether waves that were to continue to wash over us for the next decade or so. Talks, news, and the fascinating rhythm of the Savoy Orpheans (direct from the Savoy Hotel in the West End), filled our leisure moments. Great international pianists became household words and my father called Heifetz by his first name. Conversation was strictly taboo during listening hours. My mother had to wash up pianissimo and all extraneous chatter met with a cautionary 'shush!'

Sunday was a special day. From the Piccadilly Hotel, De Groot, the violinist and leader of his orchestra, played popular classics and I was permitted to stay up until 10 pm. When the novelty of listening-in had worn off for my parents I was given the free run of the set, and with the aid of a makeshift aerial in my bedroom, was able to listen in bed. Often I would fall asleep with the headphones still tightly clamped over my ears so that when mother called for me to get up and dress for school, I didn't hear her and slept on in my world of silence.

Later I discovered that the headphones could be used as a telephone with the set acting as a junction-box. A few yards of wire strung from my bedroom into the kitchen enabled my sister and me to hold long conversations and even to produce our own programmes. Under the call sign of '3LO' (the BBC had pipped us with their 2LO), we broadcast music by putting one of the headphones into the gramophone horn when a record was being played. Occasionally, some variety was added to the presentation by a violin solo played by me, with the pick-up headphone vibrating like mad on its belly. I would announce my selection in a pompous voice and scrape my way through 'Humoresque' or Schubert's 'Serenade' in a shower of falling resin.

From time to time, the crystal had to be replaced. Apart from this small item of expenditure, the set was indestructible. When the crystal was superseded by the valve, our set was honourably retired to the basement, where it survived the Luftwaffe's attempts to destroy it some thirty years later.

Rags to Riches

One of the several advantages of our life was the shopping from the itinerant barrowmen who roamed the streets from dawn to dusk, pushing their wares before them. The rattle of iron-shod wheels on the cobblestone road could be heard a mile off and the prospective customer, after a period of trial and error, could pin-point the whereabouts of any particular one of them. Fruit, sweets, fish, vegetables, ice-cream (Assenheims, they're lovely!), furniture, and even cloth, were trundled through the quarter on wheelbarrows. Each commodity was advertised in a loud, heavily accented voice. On Sundays only, a muffin man with a wooden tray balanced on his capped head and a clean white carpenter's apron tied around his waist would bawl out his wares to the accompaniment of a clanging handbell. Toasted muffins for tea was a special week-end treat that could prostrate a family with indigestion for days on end. There was also the Old Clothes man. In exchange for a bundle of garments he would present the donor with a flourishing aspidistra, or for useable items of clothing, a massive ornamental vase or half a china tea service. Almost every housewife dreamed of displaying a pair of vases on the front-room overmantel. They became a status symbol.

★   ★   ★

'The Old Clothes man is now in Gossett Street,' my mother said. 'Go take to him the bundle on top of the wardrobe in the front room.' For weeks my mother had been sorting out all the useless pieces of wearing apparel that had reached the point of no return. Frayed shirts; short trousers with patches on the patches; a torn gym-slip of my sister's beyond redemption, and several vests and long woollen underpants of my father's that had given up the ghost after years of undeniable service. All these items, and more besides, were neatly tied up in an old bedsheet, ready for disposal. I stood on a chair, took down the bundle from its lofty resting place and awaited further instructions from my mother. 'I want you should take it to Yossell the barrowman. He will give you a couple of ornaments for it. I've with him already spoken.'

Gossett Street was just around the corner past Edelstein's the tinsmith and sure enough the Old Clothes man was there. At regular intervals loud cries of 'Anyolt rags' emanating from Yossell would bring out the customers, primed to do battle for the objects of their desire.

Yossell wore a flat peaked cap which gave him the appearance of a comedian I had once seen at the London Music Hall. His badly faded blue serge suit was covered by an ill-fitting overcoat, which looked like (and probably was) salvaged out of stock. His long grey beard and steel-rimmed spectacles added a benign, short-sighted Santa Claus aspect to the comicality. I gave him the bundle. 'You're Becky's boy,' he said and opened it. In turn every item was carefully scrutinised, then thrust into a long sack at the further end of his barrow. 'Is good.' He having pronounced the verdict, I stood by to receive 'sentence'. 'The mother is wanting this pair of ornaments.' Like a magician producing rabbits out of a hat, he conjured up a pair of huge vases. They stood about two feet high with more curves on them than an undulating belly dancer. Two handles, curves within curves, were affixed from neck to belly, lined in gold and indigo. On the belly itself a pre-Raphaelite painting of semi-nude maidens, arms entwined, against a background of verdant foliage, stood admiring their reflections in a mirror-like pool at their beautiful unblemished feet. The design was framed in an oval cartouche of gold and stood out vividly against the deep blue of the main body. Both ornaments were identical.

Nervously I clutched one under each arm, and slowly made my way home praying that no mishap would befall me en route. I was perspiring freely by the time I had climbed the stairs to our flat where mother quickly relieved me of the precious burden which she carried into the front room. 'Help me tie them up', mother said. Over the fireplace we had a beautiful veneered mahogany overmantel with its delicate shelves supporting family portraits and bevelled mirrors. The cast-iron base on which it rested was covered by a scalloped green-plush curtain fringed with the same colour bobbles. It was on this mossy bank, on either side of the mantel, that the vases were put to rest. Their wide-sweeping curves thrust their bases half over the shelf edge. To prevent the imminent danger of their falling off onto the brass fender below, my mother tied them by the neck to the mirror shelves where they stood like convicted murderers waiting for the fatal drop that never came. Having assured herself that the retaining string was securely knotted, mother stood back to take in the effect. Against the polished mahogany, the blue vases achieved a sudden elegance. 'It's lovely,' said my mother proudly and walked back into the kitchen, already savouring the envy of her vase-deprived friends.

The ornaments survived for ten years, their cavernous hollow interiors being used as receptacles for money, cigarette cards, hairpins, old rent books and valuable glass marbles. I was eighteen years old when the string gave way one memorable night and the beautiful vases that mother loved, lay shattered into shapeless shards beneath the overmantel that had supported them so nobly over the years. In the fullness of time and family prosperity, they were replaced by a marble clock and a pair of rearing bronze horses. But these never attained the elegance and overripe opulence of the ornamental vases we had acquired in exchange for a bundle of cast-off clothing.

Running Repairs

Wandering through the Mittel East like figures in a medieval pageant were the itinerant craftsmen who serviced the needs of their customers with skill and promptitude. Tinkers, glaziers and chairmenders cried their calling like the muezzin from his minaret, 'Any chairs to mend?' 'Any knives to grind or pots to mend?' Voices that became familiar over the years, advancing from a brief interchange of pleasantries to the later offer of a cup of tea and a piece of yeast cake.

There was Zavel the glazier, who carried large sheets of glass anchored to a wooden frame strapped on his back together with a paintcan of putty, a glass cutter and a bottle of linseed oil. It was in summer when cricket balls were thick in the air that Zavel would materialise out of nowhere as if conjured up by a native charm involving broken glass and measure up a recently shattered windowpane with his folding boxwood ruler. Having taken the frame of glass from off his back he would find a piece nearest in size to the immediate requirement and on a square of green baize spread out on the pavement, cut it to fit. The window frame was cleared and scraped clean like a dentist preparing a cavity for a filling, and putty applied with a special knife. The new glass was pressed onto it and more putty chamfered around the edges.

Zavel spoke no English. All his business transactions were conducted in Yiddish. He lived with his family in Buross Street, a turning off the Commercial Road and was a very religious man. He would walk countless miles during each working day, his stock of glass dwindling down to a few scarcely useable off-cuts. If he'd had a good day's business he would give me a lump of putty to play with. I loved the fresh smell of linseed oil that permeated the skin of my hands and fingers. I used to model little putty animals and let them harden as the oil dried out.

Another great favourite was the tinker. Rumour had it that he was a gypsy and he was used as a figure of fright by some mothers to coerce their children into eating something not too popular with the family. 'The tinker will take you away' was a common threat that brought tears or instant obedience to mother's command. The tinker shared this distinction with the policeman and the even more frightening bogey man.

Unlike the glazier, the tinker carried all his equipment on a converted handcart. The piece de resistance was a huge circular grindstone that was mechanically turned by means of a bicycle chain and pedals which the tinker operated with his feet. Swinging from the wheel axle was an acrid smelling coke-burning brazier with the coppered head of a soldering iron buried in the glowing embers. This was ready for immediate use to patch up a leaking kettle or perforated saucepan.

There was always a job for him to do in almost every street of the quarter. He worked well into the dusk drawing up his cart under a lamp post which gave him sufficient light to carry on. In the twilight a shower of sparks would fly off the steel as the revolving grindstone rasped a ragged edge into a new sharpness. Sometimes he was so beset with repairs that he returned to the same street next day. His honesty was unquestionable. A kitchen knife or kettle, a large axe or tenon saw would be taken off home for the night, the only record being the customer's street door number chalked on the blade or tin side. Next morning he would be there working away with a file or soldering iron repairing the goods entrusted to him.

The chair mender was a specialist who plied his craft on the kerb side where, oblivious to the passing traffic, he painstakingly plaited his serpentine strips of cane to repair a chairback or seat until the frayed patch disappeared. He would sit for hours surrounded by pieces of furniture requiring his skilled attention. He also included shopping baskets in his repertoire, reweaving a handle or the bodywork that had succumbed to hard wear. When the public house on the corner opened he would go into the bar and eat his sandwich. In exchange for keeping an eye on his pitch while he was having his pint he would give me a halfpenny and a yard or two of cane fibre strips which could be twisted into spirals that slowly unwound like a tiny snake stretching itself after being coiled in sleep. When the repair was completed he would knock on the owner's door and hand over the article. He was a friendly man and didn't mind me standing over him while he worked.

Jobs for
the Boys

From the age of five until fourteen years old, children were compelled
by law to go to school. This attendance was strictly enforced by a corps
of School Board inspectors who descended on the truants with all the
legal penalties at their disposal. Only the fortunate minority of scholarship
winners stayed on past the normal school-leaving age expanding their
elementary education in the several foundation schools that flourished in
the quarter. Many of these youngsters matriculated and eventually
entered universities. There were also 'central' schools where the brighter
non-scholarship winners could learn a profession or trade and if up to
standard matriculate and go on to university.

Economic pressures in most native homes made early employment a
necessity. The average breadwinner was hard put to it to provide the
wherewithal for a fair sized family since there were too many workers
seeking too few jobs. Even the self-employed suffered the seasonal slack
times that struck the quarter with monotonous regularity. Leaving school

at fourteen with a scant knowledge of English, geography and history was not an open sesame to the aspiring wage earner who usually took the easy way out of his predicament by entering his fathers' workshop as an apprentice cabinet-maker or tailor, where over the next few years and in exchange for a few shillings a week, he slowly acquired the know-how and craftsmanship of his trade ending up as a journeyman earning about £2 10s. a week plus overtime. Nine out of ten elementary school leavers learned the trade of their father being educationally lacking to venture into the giddy heights of the Law or teaching.

It was in this field that the 'Foundation' boy had the advantage over his less endowed comrades. Matriculation was the magic key that opened the door to the Law, Accountancy, Medicine and the teaching professions with the additional social distinction of wearing a smart suit and white collar and tie to the office instead of a glue-stained apron and knotted muffler.

The Central school leaving age was sixteen. To encourage parents to keep their children at school beyond the fourteen mark the County Council awarded financial grants after a fairly exhaustive means test, the the leading questions of which were too often misunderstood by the parents of the candidates made nervous by their encounter with the authorities. At the Central school you were directed to a 'Commercial' or 'Industrial' syllabus. The former revealed the mysteries of Shorthand, Typewriting, the French language, Book-keeping and general office procedure. The Industrial section specialised in elementary engineering, draughtsmanship, Technical Drawing and Science. The normal educational curriculum which included English, History and Geography ran concurrently with both courses. Whilst the education did not come up to the Foundation standard, Central school leavers had a distinct advantage over the elementary product. Scholarships to Trade schools were available where would-be printers, builders, engineers, chefs, etc., could learn the basics of the trades in question and find jobs more readily at the end of a two year course.

All this was for the boys. Girls were limited in both scope and choice. Dressmaker, milliner, shop assistant or factory hand was the general rule. However, higher education produced better opportunities in the field of Stenography and Book-keeping, or of becoming a receptionist or telephone operator. 'She will get married soon, please God, so why waste her time in education' was the common excuse for putting a girl to work in a factory. Those girls who did manage to evade the sweatshop achieved a certain social distinction which manifested itself in a 'holier-than-thou' snobbishness that ran rife through the quarter. 'She's a clever girl, bless her; only sixteen and a shorthand typist yet', a mother would boast. For a girl to become a teacher was like the coming of the Messiah. 'Ask Mrs Goodman. Her daughter is a teacher', was status indeed. The parents basked in the adulation and vicarious glory of neighbours and the envy of close relatives.

So the young became breadwinners, putting their pittance in the family kitty and easing the burden hitherto strapped firmly on father's broad shoulders. With the weekly wage came the desire for independence with resultant conflict in the hitherto sacrosanct field of parental domination. Also the need to set up on one's own produced a proliferation of small one-man businesses run by hard-working teenagers in practically every street in the quarter. Cabinet-makers, tailors, furriers, upholsterers, crystal radio set assemblers, watchmakers and decorators all joined the endless procession of hawkers who solicited unashamedly for orders. Many of them succeeded beyond their wildest dreams and laid the foundation of some of the biggest business enterprises in the country.

Ring Up
The Curtain

Appreciation of dramatic art was usually confined to the older natives who paid sporadic visits to the Pavilion in Whitechapel Road. Here, the Yiddish theatre flourished in all its sentimental glory, offering the romance-deprived audiences improbable slices of life where virtue always triumphed over vice. At predictable intervals during each performance the actors broke into ballads that wrung the heart and brought tears to the eyes of the audience, already smarting from the pall of tobacco smoke that partially obscured the stage. Upstairs, in the overcrowded gallery, and looking amazingly like an animated Hogarth cartoon, where the mums and dads who watched the action and at the same time consumed gargantuan snacks of schmaltz herring, fish and chips, pieces of cold chicken, oranges, pineapple chunks and monkey nuts, all openly carried into the theatre in shopping baskets. The unconsumed portions of their repast were tossed over the rails onto the heads of the 'Capitalists' in the pit below. The remote verbal exchanges that followed the bombardment often provided better entertainment than the advertised play. It was here that the great Joseph Kessler hammed his way through a thousand roles, ably supporting his assorted aged leading ladies through the vicissitudes of Jewish life in the ghetto to the rapturous applause of his many fans.

But the native young found no pleasure in the sterile offerings that pleased their forebears. School acquaintance with Shakespeare and other Elizabethan dramatists had sharpened their awareness and discernment, prompting them to seek pastures new outside the quarter. Thus, Saturday nights produced a ritual exodus to the West End where the works of Shaw, Eugene O'Neil, Sean O'Cassey, and the Bard could be enjoyed for the outlay of a shilling or so.

★   ★   ★

One Saturday after lunch my mother said to me, 'Enjoy yourself, but don't come home late like last week. Daddy and me are going to Uncle Barnet'. This was my special outing to the West End. I had recently been apprenticed to a process-engraving establishment that made blocks for printers, and was now earning 17s. 6d. a week. This enabled me to indulge in the luxury of an occasional visit to the fleshpots of the metropolis where, for the expenditure of two shillings, I could see a show and indulge in coffee and chocolate eclairs at one of Lyons Corner Houses.

My friend Norman, who lived round the corner, would join me after tea and we would go into a lengthy argument as to which theatre we should patronise that night. This was usually decided by watching the buses go by on the main road. Shows were advertised on their sides. Having solved the problem to our mutual satisfaction, we would take a threepenny ride from the quarter to Piccadilly Circus and go to the gallery entrance of our particular theatre. With luck, we would be up front of the queue and settle down to a steady wait of an hour or so.

The time was passed pleasantly listening to the buskers who entertained the crowd. Songs, recitations (including Shakespeare), acrobatics, escapologists, barrel organs, and the inevitable blind beggar led by a pathetic helper, passed among us soliciting alms. With a jerk and a metallic clank the gallery door would be opened by a uniformed commissionaire, and we would pelt up the dozens of stone steps to the box-office like an avalanche in reverse. Here we paid our shillings and obtained tickets for the show. This was followed by yet another mad scramble up the remaining flights of stairs until, puffed and panting, we found ourselves at the back of the gallery barrier. Followed yet another sortie, but this time in a downward direction, in order to get a seat as near to the front as possible. We looked like a crack infantry regiment going into battle. Usually we managed to get into the centre of the first or second rows, being young,

athletic and having a good head for heights. Here, on a hard unsympathetic seat, we made ourselves as comfortable as possible, knowing full well that as the gallery filled up, we would have to shift or close up in order to make room for other people. Unless you were fortunate enough to get into the very front row, leg room was at a premium. The seats were merely cloth-padded shelves with no arm-rests in between. The man in front of you sat on your feet; you in turn, sat on the feet of the people behind. This led to a lot of harsh words and occasional kicks up the rear.

After a twenty-minute wait, the orchestra would creep into position from under the apron and tune up. We could never afford a programme so the violinist might have been Yehudi Menhuin for all we knew. Two or three popular classics were normal pre-curtain fare, usually drowned in chatter and the rustle of sweet bags and chocolate paper. Finally, to thin applause, the leader would take a bow, the house lights dim, and in the sudden and expectant silence, the curtain would slowly rise.

I saw Fred Astaire dance at the old Empire and watched young Basil Rathbone act in light comedy. Noel Coward, Gertrude Lawrence, John Gielgud, Matheson Lang, Esme Percy, Edith Evans, Sybil Thorndike, Gladys Cooper, and a host of other luminaries filled the stages of my theatreland. Occasionally an instinctive need for culture took us to the Old Vic or Sadlers Wells (a new place this), where 'early doors' were sixpence in the gallery. Charles Laughton, the Livesey brothers, Athene Seyler, and other actors of their calibre performed the works of the masters.

After the final curtain and the playing of the National Anthem, we would push our way out into the street, where the pavements were overflowing with the crowds leaving adjacent theatres. Private cars for the 'dressed' clientele and taxis for the suburbanites who panicked over the last trains to Wimbledon were waiting at the kerbside. Still excited by the show and trying to recall details of some of the highlights or a moving dramatic moment, Norman and I would push our way through the crowd like a couple of salmon swimming upstream, until we reached the Corner House facing Charing Cross Station. Here we rounded off the evening with a coffee and a plateful of creamy chocolate eclairs. Thus fortified, we would walk our way home to the Mittel East, our finances too meagre for the extra threepence fare, leaving the magic of the theatre and the bright lights of the West End behind us at the bottom of Ludgate Hill.

Frying Tonight

In an environment where joys were few and far between we made do with simple pleasures. A walk through the park with its cool soothing vistas or a visit to the local Museum, where in the shadow of past antiquities, the pressing present could momentarily be forgotten. Perhaps a nightstroll to the river with its massive iron bridges spanning the sea-weary ships that passed on the tide beneath them. Or a Sunday outing to the grey stone Tower, ringed by its empty moat like a giant vase on a hoop-la stall and patrolled by the ruff-necked custodians who tramped its historic paths. All these things and more were freely available to natives with the energy and time to spare.

But it was in the quarter itself that a deeper craving found fulfilment. Almost every district had its quota of shops that for a small outlay dispensed generous helpings of fried fish and chips. This was served onto and wrapped in old newspaper, from which the customer delicately transferred the contents to his mouth. Shops that provided unusually large portions were kept a sworn secret, their whereabouts only revealed to members of the family or the closest of trustworthy friends. For the magnificent sum of fivepence and the necessary 'know-where', a patron could enjoy the gastronomic delights of a gourmet.

★   ★   ★

'So you don't want supper', said my mother to me as I slipped on my overcoat prior to going out walking with a friend. 'Don't make a noise

177

when you come back'. I promised to be quiet as a mouse, and left. My friend Jack lived a mile away and it being a cold night, I enjoyed the brisk walk to his home where he was impatiently waiting for me at the door. On the previous evening we had arranged to eat out and Jack promised to take me to a special fish shop that served gargantuan helpings. I had sworn on my honour not to reveal its whereabouts to anyone.

We immediately set out across the quarter, like spies in a Phillips Oppenheim novel. I closely observed and committed to memory every street we passed through. This was rather difficult, since we wandered down a maze of back doubles, crossed and recrossed strangely similar roads and cut through numerous alleyways. Then the wafting fragrance of frying fish assailed my nostrils. In the surrounding gloom of an ill-lit street the shop glowed like a galaxy of stars and, appetites sharpened by the invisible aperitif, we quickened our step towards it.

A crowd was already waiting at the chest-high counter behind which the hiss and spatter of frying was clearly audible above the chatter. The shop was about twelve feet square and lit by a solitary incandescent gas mantle. Along the narrow counter-top and on a small shelf fixed to the wall immediately opposite, stood the condiments used for seasoning. Converted lemonade bottles with split corks jammed into their necks contained diluted malt vinegar. A brace of zinc salt-cellars with perforated domes and cup-type handles were tied respectively to the counter and wall by lengths of knotted string.

But it was the frying section that held everyone's interest. Here, an elderly bald-headed man, cigarette in mouth, and dressed in a dirty, once-white smock, was bent over stirring the contents of two large vats of boiling oil like a witch in Macbeth. From time to time, he would snatch up a wire basket of chipped potatoes and plunge it into the bubbling inferno. This would be followed by assorted pieces of batter-dipped fish which sizzled and fried to a golden brown. On an adjacent bench were raw pieces of cod, haddock, and fillets of plaice piled widthways beside an enamel basin containing batter mixture. As he removed the fried fish, he would rush over and dip fresh pieces in the basin and fling them in the bubbling oil which spat and spluttered angrily.

His daughter did the actual serving. She was a short, velvet-skinned, raven-haired edition of her father with the largest bosom I had ever seen in the quarter bulging under her pinafore. She stood behind a zinc-lined scuttle into which her father would soon empty the contents of the wire

baskets. Her left hand hovered over a pile of neatly-cut newsprint: her right gripped a wooden-handled scoop. With a short unintelligible grunt, the old man shot the chips into the scuttle and emptied the fish onto a wire tray. 'Who's first?' the girl shouted, picking up a half sheet of newspaper which she pressed against her ample breast, forming a crater of some considerable size into which she emptied several scoops-full of chips. A piece of fish was added and the whole neatly wrapped in a larger sheet of newsprint.

The customers in front of us were soon served and Jack and I, mouths watering, edged nearer and nearer to the counter. Soon we were next in line, pushed forward by the impatient crowd forming up behind. Fascinated, I watched the girl going through her routine of grab—press—fill—wrap, like a robot in Fritz Lang's *Metropolis*. 'Fourpenny and a pennyworth please', I ordered, and quickly collected the hot package she pushed toward me. I paid and hurried over to the shelf, where Jack joined me a moment later.

Here we carefully unwrapped our purchases to sprinkle salt and vinegar over the contents until the paper grew soggy in our hands. This was the moment supreme. Pushing our way through the crowded doorway we reached the blissfully cool air outside, leaving a tantalising astringent smell of hot vinegar in our wake. Some of the waiting customers said, 'Give us one'. In the generosity of our hearts, we permitted two or three of them to take a hot chip from our pile. It was customary to do so.

As we walked through the streets savouring our al fresco meal, Jack said, 'Didn't I tell you they give the biggest portions?' I had to agree it was so. 'It's Bessie', he continued. 'When her father serves behind the counter, everybody waits outside till she comes back. When Bessie does it against her bosom, wow!' With this final unburdening, Jack remained silent until all our fish and chips were consumed, then rolling our soggy newspapers into a ball, we played Dimmock and Clay (our current football heroes), dribbling the makeshift ball along the pavement until it disintegrated with a vinegary sigh. I never did calculate how many extra chips Bessie's ample development made possible, but I returned to the little shop in 'X' Street time and time again.

The Sound of Music

In the nineteen-twenties, culture was strictly for the 'highbrows'. Art was a school visit to the National Gallery, or the Landseer reproduction of a 'Stag at Bay' on the milkman's calendar. In the native homes, music manifested itself via the compulsory learning of the piano or violin by the firstborn of either sex. At night in Bethnal Green, scales jangled from front parlour upright grands and the cat-yowl of violins in torment added to the cacophony. The more fortunate among us possessed a gramophone whose convoluted horn, like a monstrous lily, amplified the sound and scratches of the records played on them. Continental cantors and operatic tenors were much in demand by our parents, whilst shiftless youth collected jazz. High on the hit parade were names like Sirota, Enrico Caruso, Melba and Louis Armstrong. 'On with the Motley' was the weft to the cantor's sacred warp. Apart from the do-it-yourself school of musicmakers, there were the itinerant street troubadors, who eked out a slender livelihood entertaining the passers-by or concentrating on the public bar of the local pub. Their instruments ranged from barrel organs, banjos, cornets, foot-operated harmoniums with spoon accompaniment, Japanese one string fiddles that miaowed like demented cats, and the one-man-band who played the harmonica, cymbals, drums, motorhorn and cowbells simultaneously, looking like the victim of St Vitus' Dance.

On Sunday evenings, local clubs offered cultural entertainment at a modest cost, often enticing well-known musicians to perform. Municipal parks sporting bandstands enlivened the quarter's summer with visiting regimental bands wearing colourful dress uniforms and whose polished brass instruments flashed and sparkled in the setting sun. My friends and I learned to love music and many of us, to this day, are regular concert goers. It was in centres like the Conway Hall, South Place and the Worker's Circle that we first saw the light and heard the Sound.

*   *   *

One Sunday evening my mother said to me, 'If you are going to the Worker's Circle, put on the overcoat. It's cold outside.' I called out a cheery 'Goodbye' and walked to Shoreditch Church, where I boarded a tram going to Gardiner's Corner. From there, a short walk down Leman Street brought me to Great Alie Street where the Worker's Circle huddled in the wintry dark. Inside its dimly lit vestibule the cat smell was overpowering. I walked up a flight of steps to the hall, where for the cost of a few coppers I purchased a roneoed programme which admitted me to the auditorium. As halls go, it was a tiny place, dominated by a concert grand which was the Worker's Circle pride and joy.

My fellow music lovers were cabinet-makers, tailors, furriers and pedlars. They came from Russia, Poland, Lithuania, Rumania and Germany. Yiddish was their native tongue. Many of them couldn't read the programme. Interpreters were kept busy trying to translate terms like 'largo', 'andante', or 'allegro non troppo' to eager but baffled listeners. What's the Yiddish for 'sforzando'?

Over one hundred people sat on hard uncomfortable chairs in the auditorium. They looked worried and tired. But what were a couple of hours of physical discomfort in a lifetime of misery? They waited patiently for the music to begin. The organiser introduced the eminent soloist, who bowed briefly to the applause. The ovation was not uproarious; big names didn't matter to this crowd. They judged a man by his performance

—not advance publicity. Not a soul stirred or a chair creaked while he played. They clapped late. It took a long time to come back from Beethoven to Aldgate.

It was at Circle House that I first discovered the pleasures of Chamber music. Beethoven, Mozart, Brahms, Schubert and Bach all contributed to the occasion. Many great artists played here prior to giving the same programme at the Albert or Queen's Hall. After the concert I usually walked down Whitechapel Road for a cup of coffee and cheesecake at Spielsingers.

Nocturne

Simon and Tubby lived in a tiny flat over a bank in Commercial Road. Every Wednesday during the Prom season a dozen of us gathered to hear Bach. Simon had a fine radiogram. There was a life-size bust of Beethoven on the sideboard and Low caricatures on the walls. Rose was there, too. She was a petite, with chubby arms and hands that could tear music out of any piano.

One night I walked home with Rose. It was still summer and people sat out of doors, preferring a public thoroughfare to the privacy of their furnace-hot homes. We walked through dingy streets that even the twilight could not invest with beauty. Bare brick walls with metal rivets, like giant squashed spiders, holding them together. We walked and talked and she told me about herself and music. When we got to her home, she invited me in and we went upstairs to the front room. In the dark she sat by the piano and played for me. I just sat limply listening and dreaming. I couldn't see her in the darkness: only an oblong patch of night sky above the factory wall opposite was visible. I don't remember how long I sat there listening; time didn't matter, but when I left for home, the streets were deserted and the heat coming off the pavements, stifling.

Da Capo

I was ten years old when my aunt gave me the violin. My mother said, 'Would you like to learn how to play it?', and I said 'Yes.' So she found a teacher for me. She was tall and dark, and lived two miles away. Twice a week I walked to her home with my violin safely locked in its coffin-shaped case. She taught me how to hold the bow and the names of the strings. I played scales and learned to tune correctly. When I knew my first piece, my father asked me to play it for my uncle. He gave me a sixpence and my mother was proud of me. All this was in the winter. When summer came, I heard the voices of children at play in the streets, and the violin would grow heavy in my hands. I hated to practise. My mother said, 'You must': but I hated it.

I went to another teacher, a man this time. He was fat, wore thick glasses and stared at me over them. He used to play seconds to me and I liked the harmony all right, but I still made lots of mistakes and had to keep on at the same piece for weeks. I began to lose interest and knew I wasn't cut out to be a fiddler. I liked music but didn't have the desire to play. So I told my mother, and she was very disappointed in me.

That was years ago. Since then I have regretted it a lot. It really is fine to play. I tried to carry on by myself, but there was no incentive. Sometimes at night I sit in the dark and play for hours. I play all the tunes I know and try to imagine myself giving a concert. But even to my sympathetic ears, it sounds pretty depressing.

Fortissimo

Everybody called it the Bandstand though the street plate said Arnold's Circus. Structurally it was like a gigantic wedding cake, with two layers of promenade linked by several flights of stone steps. The bandstand itself was perched on top and had a roof like an oriental sunshade. Here a brass band played on Tuesday evenings during the summer.

An hour before the performance started every seat was taken, and the crackle of peanuts combined with the shrill screams of the kids, flowed through the throng like a stampede of wild buffalo. When the band trooped in, it quietened down, but the peanut crackle continued all the evening. I loved the conductor. He had a waxed moustache shaped like a buffalo's horns, and wore a magnificent uniform that was frogged in front like that of a Ruritanian prince. The rest of the band wore uniforms too, but none so resplendent as his. After each item, the musicians shook the spittle out of their instruments. I heard 'Poet and Peasant', 'Light Cavalry' and 'The Tales of Hoffman'. I was also stunned by the brasscrash of Souza's marches. The kids cried, and giggling girls rushed through the crowd. During the interval the band would disappear into an adjacent hut, from which they afterwards emerged, wiping beer froth from their mouths and moustaches with large red handkerchiefs. We children would ask them for cigarette cards until we got a clip on the ear for our pains. When the men went back into the stand to play, we would throw handfuls of gravel at them and run off yelling.

Intermezzo

Uncle Phillip was my father's friend from Russia. He wasn't really my uncle but my father said you must respect an elderly man if you are a child, so I called him Uncle Phillip. Like my father he was a cabinet-maker. Sometimes on a Sunday my father would say, 'Let us go and see Phillip'. My sister and I were dressed in our best clothes and cautioned not to forget our manners. Together we would take the brief tram ride that separated our sector of the Mittel East from Phillip's. My sister was always sick on the tram so father used to stand on the conductor's platform with her to avoid complications. When we arrived at Phillip's house I was always pleasantly excited. He had a bound set of the *Children's Encyclopedia* which he would give me to look at. First I had to wash my hands, then he gave me the books. Phillip's son Frankie played the violin, and Debbie his daughter, the piano. He himself performed on the clarinet when he wasn't making bedroom suites in his wood-smelling workshop.

After tea, and in spite of my mother's entreaties to control our appetites we never refused any invitation to eat, Phillip would take out his clarinet from its red velvet-lined box and his son tune up the violin. In a few moments, violin, piano and clarinet would weave in harmony. The music was always sad, and my father would stop smoking and stare unseeing in front of him. My mother would cry. I quietly turned the pages of the encyclopedia. Suddenly the music would break off in mid-phrase and

Phillip would upbraid his son for playing a false note, or reduce his daughter to tears for failing to sustain a chord sufficiently. My father would self-consciously relight his cigarette and his embarrassment would be communicated to me, so that I would flick the pages of the encyclopedia until Uncle Phillip, who knew I loved music, would include me in the dressing down. When the argument was settled the music would start again and my father would sink back into his chair and listen. We would watch Phillip's anger fade away as the sound flowed true from the instruments.

Finale

Sometimes in winter when it rained during playtime, all the school was marched into the Big Hall as for morning prayers and told to sit on the floor. It was warm and dry inside, so we liked it. At the far end of the hall and facing us was the headmaster's desk. On the right of it was a bookcase containing most of the *Encyclopedia Britannica*, a couple of dictionaries and the long thin cane which the headmaster often brandished but never used. On the left of the desk and so placed that only the dark blue muslin stretched across its back was visible, was a piano. In the morning my teacher used to play hymns on it, but now it was being turned by two boys so that we could see the front. Through the noise and chatter of our excitement, the headmaster rang for silence and pleaded and coaxed for volunteers to entertain the school. A girl with long curls tied with a big black butterfly bow, stood up, and braving the storm of applause that greeted her action, walked towards the piano. The headmaster said 'Golda will now play Weber's Invitation to the Waltz'. She always did on these occasions, but our headmaster invariably announced it with a faint air of surprise that deceived us for the moment. Golda played her piece sitting straight up from the piano stool, her thin arms stilting out from her body towards the keyboard.

The next turn on the programme was Miss Jukes, my teacher, who sang about a poor soul sighing by a sycamore tree which the headmaster said was from one of Shakespeare's plays. She was a great favourite with the boys because she shook all over when she sang. After her, one of the senior lads tuned up his violin and played Czardas. I listened and envied him as he played. It looked so easy, but I knew better. As the music whirled to its swift conclusion, the applause rushed out to meet it. It took five minutes to die away, and then Mr Rossiter, the English master, asked one of the monitors to get a chair for him to stand on. He liked to sing that way so that we could all see him. Old Rosser was a tenor and it was said that he actually sang in places where you had to pay 1s. 6d. to get in. He had an Irish comic face and crisp curly hair like a negro's, only his was auburn. His songs were always jolly, and he enjoyed singing them. Unconsciously, we smiled when he smiled and frowned when he did. Old Rosser had a way with him. Behind all the music, we could hear the rain slanting against the hall windows. It was good to be inside and dry. Also the official playtime was long since over and we were cutting into our Arithmetic period. The concert lasted until going home time and included several more musical items as well as recitations involving 'The Wreck of the Hesperus' and the sad fate of 'The Boy on the Burning Deck'. When it was finally over, we stood up and said 'Goodnight teacher', and I rushed off to the gate where my mother would be waiting for me with my raincoat.

Keep Your
Fingers Crossed

Many of the immigrants came from rural communities abroad where religion and superstition were fellow travellers. Fear of the 'Evil Eye' or provoking the Angel of Death was really deep-rooted and only to be averted by incantation or guile. Any reply to a friendly inquiry concerning one's health or well-being was invariably prefaced with the magic phrase, 'No evil eye, I am well'.

Death was the supreme adversary and fought with considerable cunning. Male children were given two forenames at birth only the second of which was commonly used. The first, though known to friends and relatives, was never uttered. The object of this ploy was to keep the Angel of Death in ignorance of his intended victim's real name. Until I was a barmitzvah I never knew that my father, Maurice, was also named Jack. It was only as I was called to the torah that his full name was spoken prefaced by mine as his son.

If a button came away from my jacket or a seam undone and my mother did the sewing whilst I wore the garment, she would insist on my chewing a piece of cotton during the operation. 'Your sense will not be sewn up', she would offer as reason for the cotton. Under no circumstances would she proceed with the repair until I complied with her request.

Almost any natural phenomenon that could be interpreted as a possible danger to man had its corresponding folksy antidote. During a severe thunderstorm, mother would fill a cup with water and place it on an outside window sill where she assured me it would trap any stray thunder-bolts directed at our end of the quarter. The fact that we survived being struck down by lightning was in itself sufficient justification for her action.

In time we departed to live in West Ham (the Far East). On entering our new home mother secreted a piece of bread and a wax candle in the recess of a hall cupboard. 'So we should never be in need of food, and that life should be light in this house, please God', she explained.

Religion was a sort of magic and the rabbi a weaver of spells. 'Wonder' rabbis flourished in the Mittel East holding audience in little backstreet synagogues where, encouraged by their supporters, they delivered judge-ments or attempted to turn away the wrath of the Almighty by prayer. Most of them lived on the gratuities handed out by satisfied clients. When my youngest sister was born, mother wanted her named after our maternal grandfather Isaac. She visited a Wonder Rabbi somewhere off the Commercial Road and put the problem to him. For a cash down fee of five shillings the following ingenious solution was offered. 'Isaac', said the rabbi, 'comes from the Hebrew Yitzak meaning to laugh: laughter is happiness and happiness in Yiddish is freuden, so you will call her Freda'; and she was.

There were also certain rituals that had to be gone through associated with the wearing of new garments. 'I wish you well to wear it' or 'Use it in good health' were almost obligatory responses to the sight of new clothes. Failure to go through this routine could incur a long and pro-tracted period of intimidating silence en famille until the cause was made known and apologies offered.

Idle reference to a friend or relative's age was of necessity preceded with 'To long years' or 'Until 120'. Like the incantation against the Evil Eye it became common usage in the quarter, as did the reference to a deceased loved one always accompanied by the phrase 'May he/she come to peace'. Counting people had a built-in prohibition; it was necessary to pretend ignorance of the occasion by audibly saying 'Not-one, not two, not three, etc.' until the total number had been ascertained and dis-counted as it were. This too had a devil-in-the-background basis.

Sneezing, hiccoughs and regurgitation each had its particular safety device. Yiddish conversation was so peppered with verbal antibodies that the casual listener could easily lose track of what was being said. A failing for which my mother would have, without doubt, provided an instant orison.

189

Hearts and Flowers

Love was an emotion that a mother had for her child or children for their parents. Romance was a novel by Ethel M. Dell, in which the heroine was chastely embraced by her man against the setting sun, or a five-reel picture in the local cinema where the loving couple walked hand in hand towards the horizon, accompanied by Miss Daniels on the piano. In the native quarter it was a luxury few could afford, and then only after strict examination of tangible assets. Falling in love invariably meant trouble in the family. Can he make a living? Are her parents comfortable? Maybe he has a business of his own? In any case, what's the hurry you should get married already? Fortunate indeed were the couples who were eligible on all counts. Nevertheless, love could not be denied, nor could it be side-tracked by economics. When Spring came, mate called to mate, and soft whispers emanated from darkened doorways.

★   ★   ★

'He's got a girl, already,' my mother said to no one in particular. I was an apprentice in the printing trade at the time, and had fallen for a girl I had met at a club social. She was all my heart could desire. Tall, good-looking and lived in a large house, outside the native quarter. I began to shave regularly, dress carefully and generally behave in a manner that made it transparently obvious to my family that something unusual was afoot. Because I attended evening class each night of the working week,

Saturdays and Sundays were my only free time for social activity. My girl friend worked in a City office, too distant for a quick rendezvous during the day. In order to bridge the gap, I wrote to her three or four times a week, usually arranging a date for the weekend.

Meanwhile my parents grew curious or anxious in turn. Were her parents well off? How many other daughters did they have? etc. etc. Throughout this interrogation I would gaze unseeing out of the window, across the rooftops of the quarter. No sound penetrated the fastness of my inner self. Automatically I would make some non-committal reply, which left room for denial or admission at some later date. The sky was blue, the birds sang, and the Spring sunshine on the soot-covered brick walls transformed them into beaten gold. At evening classes where I studied art, my teacher remarked on the dash and elan with which I attacked my drawings. I lived only for the weekend when we were due to meet again.

Sometimes it was in the West End, where arm in arm, we wandered through the National Gallery, our feet echoing in unison on the polished parquet floor. Or it would be a gentle stroll through the park and around its lake, watching the energetic rowers or the match-box swans. Afterwards, it would be tea at Lyons Corner House. My girl friend would tactfully pay her own way when the occasion demanded. As an apprentice, my meagre salary did not permit the more expensive pleasures. On this count, both the theatre and cinema were out of bounds. Since she was not a native of the Mittel East, some of our most pleasurable moments were spent in exploring its back streets, or discovering the sudden little parks ablaze with tulips and tidy, neat-edged lawns, imprisoned by spearhead railings that transformed the setting into a native kraal. We would come to rest on a hard bench, conveniently away from the squalling children that shared our park with us, and speak the little nothings common to couples the world over.

At dusk we would saunter along the high street, sharing its spacious pavements with other twosomes, promenading past the shuttered shops and the ubiquitous peanut-vendor's cart where, in the hissing steam, nuts were baked to crackling perfection and sold to passers by. Later, we would enter a local cafe and order coffee and cheesecake. At that time of night the place would be crowded with natives, and the noise, overpowering, making intimate conversation impossible. Yiddish, Russian, Polish and occasional bursts of accented English, bombarded us from all sides. The painted walls with their fly-specked pictures sweated tears in the steam, cigarette smoke and heat. Our holding hands across the tea-splashed marble-topped table usually produced a knowing leer from the nearest observer. In the heat I would grow self-consciously hotter and forsake my beloved's hand, leaving it appealingly mute and forlorn on the marble.

Soon, all too soon, it was time to part. The last tram out of the quarter towards her home was imminent. We walked to the terminus and joined the waiting queue. All around us, other less inhibited couples were in close embrace, whispering endearments as they came up for air. I stood beside her, speechless. When the tram was ready to leave, I helped her up the steps and said goodnight, remaining at the stop until it was out of sight. There was always next weekend, when we would meet again, but we didn't. She became engaged to, and subsequently married, a wealthy jeweller's son, selected by her parents as a suitable mate. I believe they emigrated to Israel soon afterwards.

For one month, the sky was grey and my drawings sad and dispirited. I grew thin, morose, and took long lonely walks by the river. Shortly after vowing never to marry, I met the girl who was to become my wife. But that is another story.